# How to Be
# Your Own
# Advertising Agency

# How to Be
# Your Own
# Advertising Agency

**BERT HOLTJE**

**Illustrated by Roger Engelke**

**A James Peter Book**
James Peter Associates, Inc.

**McGRAW-HILL BOOK COMPANY**

New York   St. Louis   San Francisco   Auckland   Bogotá
Hamburg   Johannesburg   London   Madrid   Mexico
Montreal   New Delhi   Panama   Paris   São Paulo
Singapore   Sydney   Tokyo   Toronto

**Library of Congress Cataloging in Publication Data**

Holtje, Bert.
  How to be your own advertising agency.

  Includes index.
  1. Advertising.   2. Advertising management.
I. Title.
HF5823.H565   659.1   80-27207

234567890   DODO   898765432

ISBN 0-07-029665-0

The editors for this book were Robert L. Davidson and
Esther Gelatt, the designer was Roger Engelke, and the
production supervisor was Teresa F. Leaden. It was set in
Melior by Newtype, Inc.

Printed and bound by R. R. Donnelley & Sons Company.

# Contents

Preface vii

Chapter 1    Is an In-House Advertising Agency Practical?    1

Chapter 2    How to Legally Establish Your Own In-House
             Advertising Agency                              17

Chapter 3    Practical Printing and Production              31

Chapter 4    How to Save Money on All the Printing You
             Buy                                             59

Chapter 5    Tested Methods for Writing Copy                75

Chapter 6    How to Design Your Own Ads, or Buy from
             Free-lancers and Save                          105

Chapter 7    How to Plan and Manage a Media Program        123

Chapter 8    Direct Mail Techniques that Work               143

Chapter 9    How to Create Your Own Publicity and Get It
             Published                                       165

Chapter 10   Photography: How to Do It Yourself or Buy It
             for Less                                        187

Appendix     Sources of Helpful Information                 205

Index                                                        211

# Preface

Not too long ago a company that had used my advertising agency for a number of years went "in-house" for the second time. Sure, there was some loss of billing for me, and you could accuse me of munching sour grapes when I tell you that they made a big mistake. But they did it for the wrong reason. The president of the company always complained about the 15 percent commission, and even though his budget was only about $30,000, he felt that any agency should jump at the chance to do his work without a commission. Of course, he wasn't willing to pay what the creative work was worth and he didn't like the idea of a fee very much, either. I'm not defending the commission system—I think it has some serious weaknesses—but I am trying to point out that most companies go in-house for the wrong reason: economy.

The truth of the matter is that some house agencies do save their owners money. But saving money should not be the major reason for setting up an in-house agency. If instead, your goal is to do a better total communications job than is being done by your competitors, you're on the right track. And if you see a house agency giving you tighter control and direct access to the people who plan and create your advertising, you share the feelings of those who run successful live-in agencies. If you feel that in-house people are more highly motiviated and more personally interested in the fortunes of the company, you have discovered yet another secret of successful house agencies. If you save money in the bargain, it's a bonus.

Apart from showing you how to set up and run a successful house agency, in this book I have tried to point out the decisions that must be made before the step is taken. Even if you're now running a house agency, I think you'll benefit from the material presented here. Most of the house agency people I talked with in my research said that they had little contact with people in other house agencies. Many said that they would like to know how others were solving similar problems. I interviewed a lot of people for this book, and I think you'll find their comments helpful.

This is a how-to book. It contains little theory but a lot of solid information distilled from experience. But even the most elaborate book couldn't give you everything you need. You will have to talk with writers, artists, printers, and all the others who are responsible for the creation and management of advertising. To help you, I have included an appendix of practical sources.

Bert Holtje

# Chapter 1

# Is an In-House Advertising Agency Practical?

People who think that advertising agencies are hotbeds of new ideas watch too much television. Just ask anyone who uses the services of an agency what they expect, and to a man—or a woman—they'll shout, "Ideas, lots of ideas!" After all, every actor who portrays an advertising person is forever tossing off three-word headlines that make millions for the client.

But ask these same people how they prefer to pay for all these bright ideas, and they'll shout, "Commissions!"

There's the problem, and probably the reason you bought this book in the first place. But don't stop reading; I'm not going to defend the system. I'm going to show you how to get what you want without sacrificing what everyone says is inevitable when you decide to do some or all of your own advertising. Before I get into the details, though, I think you should have a clear idea of both sides of the picture.

Since you already know your side, I'll skip to the other. After all, you've probably been paying the gross amount for space ads that have been running unchanged for years and returning 15 percent to the agency every time. And, if your agency has any type of fee system, you're sure to ask yourself the same question twelve times a year: "What have they done for me lately?" Why, you may also ask, should the agency get a mark-up on all the printing they buy on my behalf? You know all this, so let's move right along.

You should know that the TV image of the busy agency bursting with ideas is a myth. It's not that most of them are not capable of it, it's just not a fact of ad agency economic life. Most agencies, no mater how creative they are, make the most money when they produce ads that are run forever in magazines that pay the 15 percent commission. If agencies had to produce ideas in proportion to the view generally held of them, and be rewarded with the 15 percent space commission, they would go broke in a hurry.

## CONSIDERING AN IN-HOUSE AGENCY

Every year someone with the credentials to do it announces that the day of the house agency has arrived. At the same time another well-qualified person tells us that the independents are the only way to go. In the years that I have been in this business, the net change from one year to the next has never amounted to a hill of beans one way or another. It's like the sweeping victories claimed by politicians after every election. If a 1 percent shift sounds like a lot, then there is a trend. But let's look at the facts.

According to a report produced by Cahners Publishing Company, in 1979, 11.6 percent of all advertising placed in specialized magazines was developed by in-house shops. That, in itself, may not seem like a lot, but they also showed that another 29.5 percent of the space placed was the result of a cooperative effort of independent agencies and in-house shops.[1] These companies were running their own advertising show, but buying some services outside. The ratio is not much different now than it was ten years ago. And I don't think it will be much different ten years from now.

However, Ron Coleman, managing director of the Business/ Professional Advertising Association, had some news that may accelerate the house agency trend. According to a report published in *Advertising and Publishing News* in November 1978, 56 percent of the respondents to a survey said that they intended to increase their amount of in-house activity in sales promotion over the next five years, and 53 percent said that they would go in-house for product publicity, trade shows, and sales support material in the next five years.[2]

The report also showed that many respondents were unhappy with their agency's way of pricing printing and other services. However, most agreed that it definitely was a mistake to evaluate advertising strictly in terms of price alone.

So, what's the point? It's just this: A good case can be made for any point of view. Whether you go in-house, use some outside services, or leave everything up to an independent agency depends mainly on how much you are willing to undertake yourself. It also depends on how capable your in-house people are compared with the services you can buy from an independent agency, or specialized services. The decision can't be made on price alone. Anyone can choose the lowest bidder, but it takes some thought to choose the system that will be best for you in terms of economics as well as productivity.

## THE ECONOMICS OF RUNNING AN AGENCY

People decide to handle their work in-house for many reasons. Despite the press releases that tell of "mutual agreements" to terminate agency contracts, the decision usually boils down to economics. Of course, there are times when an agency just does bad work. But these shops seldom survive, so let's look at the economic side of the story.

Most industrial advertisers place more fractional space than full-page ads. And they probably use more quarters than any other size. Let's use this size for our discussion. The average quarter-page ad in a nationally circulated trade magazine costs about $600 (in 1980). The 15 percent commission puts $90 in the agency's pocket every time the ad runs. Let's further assume that the average manufacturer's space-advertising budget is $20,000. When this is spent, the agency will have collected a total of $3,000 in commissions. For this, they are expected to do all of the media planning, placement, traffic, and account management, but none of the creative work. Some advertisers still think that the agency should be paid for its creative effort out of the commission, but the average industrial ad budget just isn't large enough to support the work.

To most advertisers this seems like a lot of money. But to most agencies, it represents only enough to keep the doors open, assuming there are enough $20,000 clients in the shop. I'm not going through this to tell you how tough it is for an agency to make a buck handling industrial clients; I'm doing it to give you a picture of what you can expect when you act as your own agency. Stay with me—it does get better.

Next, suppose that you spend another $20,000 on catalogs, product-data sheets, and other printed promotional material. About one-quarter of this will, or should, be spent for the creative work. If you spend less on the creative work, the chances are that your work will look like everybody else's. And that's pretty bad. If you buy your creative work outside, buy the best you can. The best usually costs more, but it may not necessarily be the most expensive. (More on this in other chapters.) For now, though, I want to show you what happens when your outside agency buys printing and what you can expect when you take over.

Every agency has its list of favored suppliers—the printers, typesetters, statmakers, and photographers on whom they depend. These people offer their highly creative and very personal services in much the same way as others sell nuts and bolts. Buy a lot from them and they'll give you a discount. It's nothing unusual, just good business. If a printer knows he can depend on a lot of business from one source, he knows that his selling cost will be less than if he had to keep scurrying for new business. Therefore, to protect this steady business, he offers better prices.

The smart agency production person shops around until he or she finds the suppliers that meet the agency's quality standards and are willing to negotiate favorable prices.

When an agency buys printing for its clients, it tacks on a markup and rebills the client. The price that the agency charges usually is about what the advertiser would pay retail. However, most agencies really do quite a bit of work for this markup. First, the agency that buys printing on behalf of its clients assumes responsibility for the job. If the printer blows it, it's up to the agency to hassle the printer for a rerun or to have the bill torn up. Of course, some agencies do not markup printing; they pass along the printer's bill as is. These shops negotiate a fee for shepherding the job through all of the printing and production stages. They are payed for the work they do, not for the amount of printing that the client buys.

The agency that pays your printing bills and marks up the cost is expected to check and release the proofs, and supervise the job from start to finish. If you're dealing with an elaborate four-color job, the markup may be well worth it. But for the routine jobs, it may be worthwhile for you to become printing-smart. Of course, it all depends on how you see yourself spending your time.

As I mentioned, printers who feel they can count on a lot of steady work from a few sources will charge less per job. Every printer who knows his profit-and-loss picture clearly has to figure in a selling cost, whether or not he employs a salesperson. If a lot of work comes in with very little selling effort, the printer is usually willing to knock off a few points. But how much is a few points? I wish I could tell you, but no two printers work the same way, and every situation has its own individual elements. So the best advice I can give you is to get estimates from several printers, telling each exactly what you are doing, and giving an accurate picture of your anticipated future volume. Remember, there are printers who will throw you a low ball to get the first job. They'll make up the loss on future work, if you're not careful. This tactic becomes obvious when you're honest with the printers you talk with. However, be sure that all the printers in the race for your work have essentially the same capabilities, skills, and equipment. The last thing you want is the lowest bid from a printer with a small press who wants to do 100,000 copies of your 400-page catalog. The price may be right, but your products will be obsolete by the time the catalog is printed.

## WHAT QUESTIONS TO ASK

A lot of problems never seem to have definite solutions. The question of whether to use an in-house or independent agency is one. The decision is made when it *appears* that one way is better than another. However, in getting to this point, most people ask the same questions. Robert Pulver, who runs the in-house advertising operation for General Electric, in Stamford, Connecticut, tackled this problem in an article in *Industrial Marketing*.[3] Pulver knows what he's talking about, and even though he runs one of the most respected in-house operations in the business, he presents both sides clearly. Here are the comments he claims are most often heard when an in-house agency decision is in the offering.

**In-House**

We know our business.

We can turn around faster because we control the resources.

We can deal with confidential information.

We're loyal; we have only our company's interest at heart.

We can save 15 percent.

You only care about your own profits, not ours.

**Independent Agency**

We know the advertising business.

We can turn around faster because we're competitive and hungry.

We can attract and hold creative talent.

We're objective; we do what's right, not what's political.

We can make the other 85 percent work harder.

You only care about building a personal empire.

As you can see, there are no pat answers that apply to everyone. However, if you use this as a checklist when you investigate both options, I'm sure you will have an easier time of it than if you don't.

## FINANCIAL STRATEGY

Since most companies start their in-house agencies for economic reasons, let's look at financial strategy now. Even if you are going to use people who are already on the payroll, there are a few decisions you should make before you go any further. It's a serious mistake to assume that employees whose assignments leave them with some free time can run your house agency. Even if they pass the matchbook art test, it's not a good idea to confer the title of art director immediately. Going in-house is serious business, and you should plan for it just as carefully as you would if you were adding an R&D department or putting up a new building.

Some companies treat their in-house shops as overhead, and others charge costs directly to the departments within the company that use agency services. Whichever method you choose, I strongly advise that you set it up on a strict accounting and accountability basis. Know how much you are spending, how much you are saving, and how effective the work is compared with work that would have been done by an independent agency. This is a tough order, but it should be done.

Many house agencies are given profit-and-loss responsibility. However, most of the shops don't aim for a profit; they shoot for a break-even point. This approach tends to reduce the possibility of a sloppy operation. You could end up spending more in-house than you did when you used an independent agency if you are not careful. You may not like the prices charged by independents, but if they have survived for a few years, they do know how to stay in the black. Unless you operate with the same philosophy, you may be fooling yourself. The GE in-house agency covers costs through a combination of media commissions, markups, fees, and time charges. None of the costs are in company overhead.

In addition to strict financial accountability, you should establish real goals for your in-house agency. It's not enough to say that a new catalog must be printed and a few new ads prepared. The plan should have specific objectives that are tied directly to your marketing and financial plans. If you are spending $25,000 on a new catalog, for example, decide just how much new business it should produce. If you can't justify the cost, adjust the program or the sales estimate so that the money spent will produce a suitable profit. But this is nothing new (I hope); you should have been doing this with your independent agency all alone.

## WHAT ABOUT PEOPLE?

Until now, most of the answers have been easy. But when it gets down to people, your real problems begin. It's generally true that most creative people tend to gravitate to the independent shops. These people like the variety provided by working on a number of different accounts in an independent agency, and feel that this stimulation may be lacking in an in-house shop. They also feel there is more room to grow and the opportunity to make more money with independent agencies.

However, there are many very creative people who dislike the gnawing insecurity that exists in most agencies. Lose an account one day and lose your job the next. It's a fact of life in most agencies and a fact you can trade on when you recruit people for your in-house shop. If you are running recruitment ads or doing personal interviews, stress stability and you will probably be flooded with applicants.

According to Robert Pulver, general manager of the General Electric house agency, "Getting good creative talent is more difficult and it really depends on what the talent is looking for in a job. The ones who like to participate in the whole marketing process and see how advertising plays its part are the ones who like the in-house environment."[4] He also feels that greater job stability is a big plus. However, this could also mean that companies are more reluctant to fire a person who doesn't perform. One way out of this problem is to set up an entirely separate advertising agency, complete with its own salary and benefit structure. This arrangement will also help solve the problem of the stifling corporate environment that often makes advertising people unwilling to work in an in-house situation.

## Do Creative People Go Stale Working In-House?

One of the most common fears is that creative people can go stale quickly when working only on a limited line of products or services produced by the parent company of the in-house agency. This is a very real problem, but it is by no means insurmountable. Some companies have solved it by taking on outside advertising clients, not only to provide the creative stimulus, but also to pick up some of the freight if the house agency is not yet cost-effective. Others rotate the work assignments so that there are periods of concentration for each individual, rather than a general exposure to all the products all the time.

W. D. Woodburn, president of Advertising Directions, the Santa Fe Industries house agency, told me that he solves the problem by drawing upon outside talent. He said, "The one risk of an in-house operation is in creative output. It is almost impossible to compete with top dollars paid by full-service agencies for talent in the creative field. However, we overcome this difficulty by using free-lance talent on a project basis."

Many of the poeple I talked with who run in-house operations have solved the problem of getting top creativity by turning to outside services, such as individual free-lancers, and specialized boutiques, and even by using services of full-service agencies on an à la carte basis.

Several people felt that the head of an in-house agency has the problem of trying to serve two masters. As head of the agency and an employee of the client, they said it is difficult to provide the objectivity and goal-oriented leadership necessary to do the best job. However, if goals and job responsibilities are clearly defined, this should never become a problem. Whether the person is on the payroll of the client as president of the house agency, or is on the payroll of an outside agency, the same objectivity must exist. The individuals as well as their work should be subject to the same criteria whether the work is done in-house or by an outside full-service agency.

## THE CHARACTERISTICS OF SUCCESSFUL IN-HOUSE AGENCIES

Milo Ziegenhagen, a Connecticut based marketing communications consultant, feels that potential do-it-yourselfers should compare their objectives with those who run successful in-house shops. According to Ziegenhagen, a lot depends on *why* the house agency is wanted.

Ziegenhagen claims that those who have pulled it off didn't do it to save money, get into the advertising business, or even to improve the effectiveness of their advertising. They may have accomplished all of these things, but these were not the immediate goals. He feels that the strongest motivation is to beat out competitors in every facet of marketing communications, field sales support, and marketing.

When I spoke with him, Ziegenhagen revealed the three characteristics he feels are shared by most successful companies that run in-house agencies.

1. The companies are medium to large in size. It's more difficult to justify the expense for a small company, and smaller companies probably haven't faced the problems that help push larger ones into the house-agency business.

2. The companies have an integrated operating style. That is, if there aren't fairly well-enforced companywide policies that go beyond bottom-line management, the chances of success are slim.

3. The chief operating officers are willing to stand up for a program of high standards for all marketing communications.

One person who feels that his company meets these requirements is George Dixey of Blue M Electric Company, Blue Island, Illinois. He said, "We have operated a successful in-house agency since 1964. By successful I mean we create all our trade paper ads and place them, create all our own promotional material (everything from single-page flyers to 200-page, two-color catalogs), and create and implement a continuing direct-mail program. In short, we do virtually everything an external agency does. And by we, I mean two people—a secretary and me."

Mr. Dixey also mentioned some of the benefits he feels accrue to his operation: "You know that you won't go over budget since you control it absolutely. You know that there'll be money to spend in December just as there was in May. You know what a printing job will cost. There are no hidden extras, no surprises. And you know what the finished piece will look like because (like everything else) you control it."

Rich Young, who has run a house agency at The Badger Company for more than two years, feels that little attention has been paid to house agencies because it's not in the best interest of the media. Rich said, "Unfortunately, this area [house agencies] is unexplored because publications don't want to appear supportive of any action that may kill the fatted calf. I believe that there are companies that should go in-house while others are better off having a full-service agency. Each situation has to be evaluated separately."

The Badger house agency is, indeed, a productive operation. Rich Young works with only one assistant, a communications coordinator, and a secretary. With this staff of three, and the services of two free-lance artists and a free-lance writer, he manages to handle all space advertising, public relations, audio-visual programs, sales literature, and trade shows, and he has had about twenty-five technical articles published each year.

The Badger operation makes no pretense at being anything but a house agency. "We never even formed a paper agency," Young said. Very few of the publications gave him any trouble with the commission, and those that did soon came around.

However, Rich feels that the problem of objectivity exists and is best handled by working with outside creative people.

"The 15 percent wasn't our major reason for going in-house," Young said. "We used an agency for twenty years that served us well, but it went bankrupt. The agency we chose as a replacement provided slow service, was not responsive to our needs, and gave us consumer copy for our industrial services. They claimed that they were a full-service agency and could do everything, but, in fact, they couldn't. I found it almost impossible to know whether or not they were making the best buys on our behalf on such items as printing. Running your own in-house shop provides a keen sense of cost control that is missing with many outside agencies."

## SURVEY IDENTIFIES CRITERIA FOR SUCCESS

Rick Braithwaite, Advertising Manager for the Information Display Division of Tektronix, Beaverton, Oregon, has worked on both sides of the fence and has conducted extensive research on house agency usage. Rick surveyed 357 advertisers across the country and came up with some interesting insights for those who are on the fence.[5]

Rick found that companies using in-house agencies are more likely to determine their advertising budgets by using the objectives method than those who use independents. Those who use full-service agencies lean to budgets prepared as a percentage of sales. It appears that the reason for this is that in-house agencies are much closer to the marketing functions of the company, which results in better communications and more accurate, in-depth budget planning.

Braithwaite's research showed that in-house agencies are more prevalent in small and medium-size companies, those with fewer than 5,000 employees. Of course, many much larger companies use in-house services, but the survey did more to indicate a trend rather than to make an absolute statement.

The survey also indicated that the more sophisticated the method of advertising, the more likely the company was to rely on outside services.

When asked how they evaluate the services of an outside agency, many of the respondents preferred to review the agency's creativity and ability to develop sales leads.

One of the most revealing questions asked about the method of compensation used with full-service agencies. The answer gives some insight into the commission versus fee dilemma. According to Braithwaite's report, "Commissions and a combination of fee and commission are more common in firms with over 1,000 employees than straight fee compensation plans." It appears that larger companies do more space advertising and the agencies they employ can make their money on media commissions. Braithwaite said, "Smaller firms will spend more of their advertising money on collaterals and smaller media schedules, so agencies are forced to charge fees for services to cover their expenses." This is in concert with what most people I interviewed said.

Another trend Braithwaite noticed is that "Commissions, either by themselves, or in a combination with fees, are not used by those companies using full-service agencies, and which employ fewer than 100 employees. The reason is fairly obvious. They are probably such small advertisers that commissions on media advertising (if any) would never begin to cover the costs the agency incurs. Therefore, they have set up some sort of retainer or fee per job relationship that provides the agency with profit, and the company with cost-effective advertising."

When asked, "If given the choice, would you create an in-house agency? " Braithwaite got answers that led him to summarize the feelings of the respondents this way:

> Surprisingly enough, over one-quarter (29 percent) of the respondents indicated that an in-house agency might be used in the future. The most common reason seems to deal with a more efficient communications link between the company and agency personnel that would result in better control. Cost savings was also considered important, but to fewer companies than most full-service proponents might expect. Reasons against include sixteen responses that the in-house agency concept wouldn't work because the company isn't large enough to handle the overhead, not because the concept itself is no good. The other responses indicate a dislike for the in-house concept and strong feelings that they would not work for the respondent's company.

The study also showed that as the size of the in-house agency grows, they are more likely to use additional outside services for some of their advertising efforts. This apparent paradox can be explained by the more sophisticated requirements of the larger firms. The small firms with small in-house operations usually limit their activity to pretty basic work. However, the needs of the larger firms are better served by the talents and abilities of people who are either free-lance consultants or can be bought on an à la carte basis from full-service agencies.

Perhaps the most telling answers were given to a question that asked for the greatest advantages of an in-house agency. Braithwaite summarized his findings by saying:

> The greatest advantage of in-house agencies is their grasp of product and market information. In contrast, only 8 percent [of the respondents to the question] of those who used full-service agencies indicated better product and market knowledge as the reasons they would switch to an in-house agency. The importance of cost savings to those using in-house agencies is much less than it is to those using full-service agencies, but indicating a desire to switch to in-house. Only 20 percent indicated it as the greatest advantage in the in-house category, while 39 percent said it was significant in the full-service group. This indicates that the in-house agencies are not as economical as many think, or that more important advantages than cost savings are realized.

## IN-HOUSE OR INDEPENDENT AGENCY?

So far, I have introduced you to quite a few people with fairly strong opinions. And I'm sure that you have noticed that I have avoided telling you that you should go one way or the other. Don't chalk this up to indecisiveness, or to the fact that I make my living running an advertising agency. The reason is this: There is no way that I, or anyone for that matter, can make that decision for you. It's a decision that must be based entirely on your own needs, the needs of your company, and how you see these needs being filled. I am convinced that there are many companies that could benefit considerably from an in-house agency, and there are others with in-house shops that should get rid of them. One client I had twice tried the in-house route strictly for economic reasons. In both cases, the owners saved some money, but they turned out some pedestrian advertising.

## The Case for a Full-Service Agency

John Monsarrat, in a pamphlet for the American Association of Advertising Agencies, summed up his case *for* the outside, full-service agency this way:[6]

1. Centralization of responsibility of accountability
2. Simplified coordination and administration
3. Greater objectivity
4. Sales-oriented creative work
5. Synergistic experience
6. Stronger pool of talent
7. Historical importance of full-service agencies to business success
8. In some cases, less expensive
9. Simplified corrective change
10. Better working climate and espirit de corps

## The Case for an In-House Agency

Rick Braithwaite summed up the reasons for an in-house agency in another report this way:[7]

1. Cost savings
2. Superior service
3. More responsible and dedicated to corporate needs
4. More efficient
5. Improved speed
6. Better grasp of company's products and markets

If you have been following me, I think you will have noticed that those for and those against house agencies have used many of the same arguments to make their points. But, I think that the most important point I can make is that the success of an in-house agency can't be predicted, nor can the decision to go in-house be made the same way by everyone. In-house agencies do work, and outside full-service agencies can provide good service at reasonable prices. As several of the people I've quoted have said, it appears to be more important why you want to go in-house, than how you do it. However, once you decide to do it, you will have to know how to do it. And, assuming that you have decided to handle some or all of your advertising and promotion inside, that's what the rest of this book is all about. Now let's look at the legal aspects and the form of agency that will be best for you.

## Notes

[1]*Cahners Advertising Research Report*, no. 102.1, Cahners Publishing Co., Boston, Mass., 1979, p. 1.

[2]Don Baines, "Build advertising around your customer's wants," *Advertising & Publishing News*, November 1978, p. 29.

[3]Robert Pulver, "Advertising Services—Make or Buy?" *Industrial Marketing*, July 1978, p. 72.

[4]Ibid., p. 74.

[5]Rick Braithwaite, "Investigation into the In-House versus Full-Service Advertising Agency Situation in the United States," unpublished report, California State University, Fullerton, 1977, p. 14.

[6]John Monsarrat, "The Case for the Full Service Agency," American Association of Advertising Agencies, New York, 1971.

[7]Rick Braithwaite, "An Evaluation of the Utilization of In-House Advertising Agencies in America: As Reported in Major Advertising Periodicals for the Years 1965-1976," unpublished report, California State University, Fullerton, 1977, p. 17.

# Chapter 2

# How to Legally Establish Your Own In-House Advertising Agency

Despite almost universal acceptance by the media of house agencies, the question most frequently asked by would-be do-it-yourselfers is, "Is it legal?" Not only is it legal, it's quite respectable. In fact, some of the biggest and most successful house agencies share the same roof with some of the biggest and most prestigious companies. The reason you don't hear much about these live-in arrangements is that those who run them are usually too busy attending to business to blow their own horn.

Robert Pulver, general manager of GE's house operation, said, "The people who run in-house organizations have their own fish to fry and aren't likely to give you a lot of time."[1] This is very true. I talked with many people who run in-house shops, and while all were cordial and very helpful, most were more interested in doing what they do best: advertising. However, those who run full-service agencies have to think about business development as well as the creation of advertising. Therefore, much has been published about independent agencies, and little about house agencies. Even though 11.6 percent of all space placed in business publications in 1979 was developed by house agencies, and another 29.5 percent was placed by house agencies with outside help, you seldom hear anything about them.

Rich Young, manager of The Badger Company's house agency said in a letter to the editor of *Industrial Marketing*, "I'd like to hear from those who have successfully gone in-house."[2] The response to his request was heavy from those with house shops as well as from those who were thinking about it. Many of those who are on the fence are concerned with the legality; it seems they feel that running a house agency is at worst illegal, and at best immoral. It's neither, but to understand why, you should know how this mess of commissions and agency recognition got started.

## HOW IT ALL BEGAN

In the latter half of the nineteenth century when newspapers began to expand beyond their local circulation, advertising agencies came into being and undertook the sale of space for a commission. When companies began to distribute their products nationally, they had to find ways of reaching the newspapers that would be of value, and the commission agencies did the job.

These early agencies were really space jobbers, or independent space brokers, who sold space for many newspapers and were given a commission by the publishers. They didn't write copy or do artwork; they just peddled space.

It wasn't too long before these entrepreneurs saw that they could make even more money by buying the space themselves in large lots at hefty discounts. They then sold the space in smaller lots to advertisers, negotiating their own deals somewhere between the discount price they paid and the published line rate. It was at this point that the agencies began to offer the creative and marketing services for which agencies are known today. The manufacturers who advertised in many papers all over the country needed the help of writers, artists, media people, production people, and all the others who now make up the staffs of modern agencies.

Oddly enough, the organization that many people consider to be the prototype of the modern advertising agency was, in fact, a house agency. In the 1890s, Lever Brothers set up shop because they felt they couldn't get the advertising help they needed elsewhere. The Lever shop employed writers, artists, and production and research people, much the same as a modern full-service agency. Actually, the house agency was the dominant force in the business until the turn of the century.

In the 1920s, when newspapers and magazines expanded way beyond their local circulation bases and radio broadcasting came into being, independent advertising agencies really began to flourish. Many of the original house agencies stayed in business, but this was the period of greatest expansion for the full-service independent agencies. In fact, when Warner Lambert opened a house agency to handle Listerine, its decision was criticized heavily by the business press.

When television became the heavy medium, the advertising business expanded even more, but there was little shift one way or another in the house agency picture. However, in the 1960s a shift to house agencies became apparent. No one knows for sure why this happened, but most people feel that the availability of topnotch free-lance talent as well as economic pressures can be credited with the trend.

During this time, the master served by the independent advertising agency had changed completely. Originally the agencies worked for the publishers—they were agents in the legal and practical sense. Now, however, advertising agencies work for advertisers and should really be called advertising *services* to avoid the legal problem implied by the word agency. However, the commission compensation system of the nineteenth century still haunts the house shop as well as the independent full-service agency today.

In the late 1800s, when agencies sold space for publications on a commission basis, they were given a 25 percent commission. By 1891, the rate had dropped to 15 percent, and there was a time between 1912 and 1917 when the figure was 13 percent. However, since 1918 the standard rate of commission for

publication space has been 15 percent. Under any other circumstances it would be very unusual for an agent acting on behalf of
a principal to receive commissions from the other partner to a
contract, in this case, the publisher. However, according to law,
if the principals are aware of the situation and agree to allow the
agency to receive the commissions, there is nothing illegal about
the relationship. Even though most advertisers and their agencies seldom discuss this fact, the implied agreement is generally
enough in the eyes of the law.

The early full-service agencies gave away the creative work.
In those times, the commission granted by the publications not
only covered costs, it turned a tidy profit for the pioneers.

Today, however, most agencies cling to the 15 percent, yet
must make other charges in order to make money. Gary Lewis,
manager of advertising for Steelcase, Inc., Grand Rapids, Michi-
gan, said in an article he wrote for *Industrial Marketing*, "Media
commissions on relatively low cost space don't compensate the
agency on the account."[3] He's right, but 15 percent goes a lot
farther on the big consumer accounts where television and color
advertising in major consumer publications can add up to a lot of
money. As I've mentioned before, the money saved on the 15
percent commission is seldom enough to justify the switch to a
house agency for most small to medium-size industrial
advertisers.

## COMMISSIONS AND/OR FEES

Why is everyone so uptight about the 15 percent commission? Largely, I suspect, because it comes from the publisher, a
third party, and isn't directly related to the services performed.
Most advertisers, when they complain about the commission
system, say that they feel the agency is getting the 15 percent for
nothing. However, they don't realize that the price charged by
the agency for the creative, production, and traffic work that
leads up to the placement of an ad is seldom sufficient without
the commission. The agency is betting that the ad will run often
enough so that the 15 percent commissions will add up to
enough money to repay them for their work.

Oddly enough, many advertisers are more aware of the problem than the agencies give them credit for. It's often the agencies that are too shy to speak up for the true value of their services. If they did, a fee system would be much more popular today, and it would be more beneficial to both parties than the blackjack game of 15 percent commission.

A survey conducted several years ago showed that fee arrangements were most common with industrial companies spending under $1 million. The fee arrangements came about largely at the request of the agencies, but very few agencies are currently using a fee system.

A fee system can be used in many ways. For example, when an agency works on a 100 percent fee arrangement, all the space commissions are credited to the client's account. Because the fees will always amount to more than the commissions, there is little likelihood that a publication will call it rebating and clamp down on the space it sells to the agency. In theory, a publication will not give a commission directly to an advertiser, but none has ever refused to grant a commission when the client is on a 100 percent fee system.

Many people feel that the 15 percent actually works against the best interests of the advertisers when an outside agency is involved. They feel that the advertiser is paying for advertising by dollar volume, and not for creative work. However, as I mentioned in the opening pages of this book, most small to medium-size advertisers want top creative work, but feel that their space commissions should cover the cost.

I realize that all this sounds like an advertisement for your local full-service agency. In a sense, it is. But only to help you see both sides of the picture clearly. However, as I've also mentioned, the decision to go one way or another should not be made on the basis of saving the 15 percent, it should be made to give you the best advertising at fair prices. You can get this from an independent as well as in-house, and before you decide to take the plunge strictly on the basis of the money saved, you might think about working with your present agency on a fee basis. In effect, you can have your cake and eat it too.

Some agencies that use a fee system estimate their costs in advance, and then add 25 to 30 percent for profit. All purchases made by the agency for the client, such as typography, photography, printing, etc., are then billed at cost. The fee that is charged includes all direct costs, overhead, and profit. Agencies that work this way review the structure with their client regularly to insure that it is working favorably for both parties.

As practical, neat, and simple as this may seem, most small to medium-size industrial advertisers are afraid of the system. They still feel that the agency should receive its compensation for all of its work by way of the 15 percent commission. Under the best of circumstances, there is seldom enough billing to make this workable for the agency. And most advertisers juggle their advertising program during the year, seldom spending all they budgeted for. When the agency's income is riding on this juggling act, you can see why the principals of most independent industrial advertising agencies are a nervous lot. If the space schedule is cut, the agency is the loser.

That's the gist of the 15 percent nightmare advertisers and agencies live with. If you wonder why I took you through this background, it's to put the agency business into economic perspective. After all, if you are going to open a house agency, you are going into the agency business with yourself as client. And, if you're going to run an agency, you had better know how to charge yourself or you will wish your old, commission-grabbing agency would come back and take the monster off your hands. As you are going to see, it's not simply a matter of dreaming up a name and sending your own insertion orders. You are going to have to run your house agency the same way you run your business. You're going to have to set up books, monitor your efforts and expenses, and generate a P&L statement. I assure you that it can work, but you're going to have to work to make it work.

## HOW TO FORM AN IN-HOUSE AGENCY

In 1956, Consent Decrees were signed by the American Association of Advertising Agencies, American Newspaper Publishing Association, and other industry organizations in which they agreed to no longer deny commission to house agencies. However, nothing prevents each medium, acting in its own interest, from denying commissions. But this is seldom done unless there is a blatant attempt to collect commissions without doing the work that would have been done by an independent agency.

Some who have formed house agencies took all the steps necessary to set up legally recognized organizations, while others have simply given a name to their advertising department, which does full-service advertising work for its employer.

George Dixey, who runs the house agency for Blue M Electric Company, took the latter route. "And, I did not create a paper agency just to make it look as though an agency is handling the account," he said when he described his operation. He has operated a very successful house agency since 1964. "But it's risky," he said. "Make no mistake. How do you know, for example, that the last ad was the best it could have been? Could someone else (on the outside) have done it better? With better results? You wonder, but you never know."

Fred Tipple told a group of advertising people at an American Management Association meeting how he created a house agency, Advertising Directions, Inc., as a corporate affiliate of Sante Fe Industries:

> In a multi-company operation, we decided that the best plan for Santa Fe was to form the agency as an affiliate company within the framework of the total organization. Our Santa Fe agency operates as a profit center handling advertising for all the parent company's operations. This type of operation conforms to the requirements of the media who follow certain guidelines in meeting their recognition for the 15 percent commission. Our affiliate company is set up like most full-service advertising agencies and can compete for any number of clients we think can be served effectively through our operations. Compared to an affiliate advertising company, the in-house agency is usually not a separate company and the format varies to fit the requirements of a specific corporation and their advertising requirements.[4]

However, the ad agency must do more than be a legal entity to collect the 15 percent. About this, Tipple said in his address, "When a company prepares their advertising for media in a professional manner and the company has a good credit rating, the media will allow the commission, provided the billing is not made direct to the company."

Often an in-house agency is a complete advertising department that does all of the work that would be done by an independent agency. But, as Tipple noted, "They must have a separate identity which is a created name for billing purposes."

Oddly enough, even some of the larger trade magazine publishers, who are in a position to withhold commissions from in-house agencies, have in-house agencies for their own promotional efforts. Some try to look straight by placing their own advertising through independent agencies, but these open secrets are well known.

I have stressed the need to run a tight ship when you start a house agency. It's easy to get sloppy when the parent company makes money, and doesn't care very much whether the agency is in the black, or not. Tipple commented on this, too, in his address:

> The advertising department personnel must either change hats and become agency people or they wear two hats—one as a member of the agency and the other as a member of the advertising staff. In either case, there must be a division of operations for each person on the staff. Usually a time study will reveal what percentage of work should be charged to the agency and how much to the advertising department. If you don't make a study of this type, you cannot properly evaluate the benefits or problems of the agency operation.

GE's Pulver feels strongly about this, too. Referring to a conference he had attended, he wrote, "One thing that all of us at the conference agreed on was that no matter how you cover your in-house costs, you need a solid cost-accounting system that analyzes all the direct, indirect, and overhead costs."[5]

An affiliate company is a legal entity, not just a name hung on the group that creates your advertising. Either your staff counsel, or an outside attorney, should take the necessary steps to create the company within the structure of the parent. It's not a big deal, but if you're going to take this route, get good legal advice and do it right. Also, talk with your accountants. The questions of capitalization, insurance, and local licenses should be answered before you go into business. The question of finances may be a hang-up with some media. However, if you can show that you (the parent company) have sound credit, most media will grant the commissions without question—as long as you do the job that would have been done by an independent agency.

## HOW TO GAIN MEDIA RECOGNITION FOR YOUR HOUSE AGENCY

Prior to the signing of the Consent Decrees in 1956, gaining recognition was somewhat like admittance to a secret order. Nobody had to learn a secret handshake, but a lot of mystery attended recognition. Actually, the publications wanted to make sure that the agencies were good for the money they were planning to commit for clients, and they didn't want to bite the agency hands that fed them. Rich Young of The Badger Company summed it up for me: "Unfortunately, the area is unexplored because publications don't want to appear supportive of any action which may kill the fatted calf."

People still speak reverently about agency recognition, but it's nothing more than acknowledgement that you have assured the media that you can pay your bills and will supply advertising in a professional manner. Broadcast media do individual checks on the clients and agencies who buy time because of the large sums that are often involved. But because there are so many small to medium-size industrial advertisers, recognition is left to several trade associations. The American Newspaper Association obviously handles newspapers and the Periodical Publishers Association is responsible for consumer magazines. Most of you reading this book will be evaluated by the American Business Press or the Agricultural Publishers' Association. The print media served by the groups provide recognition as long as the agency has been approved by the credit rating service of these groups. That's all there is to it, except to remember to pay your bills on time!

## THE PROBLEM OF LIABILITY

When an advertiser uses an outside agency to place its space, the agency agrees to pay the publisher the net amount, which is the stated rate less 15 percent, and bill the client the gross amount for the space. If the agency goes under or doesn't pay the bills, or if the client refuses to pay the agency when the agency has already shelled out the cash, nasty lawsuits usually result.

Whether your house agency is little more than a paper department or a legally constituted affiliate company, the problem of liability is important. The media tend to use sole liability clauses in their contracts that hold the advertising agency liable for the space bought. This shields the advertiser from a lot of claims that may be made if problems arise. It also reduces bookkeeping problems for the advertiser. Only one check for all space bought in a specific period need be written to the agency. The agency, in turn, pays each individual publication.

Even though the agency must write a bundle of checks each month, it has the very real advantage of being able to write these checks for net amounts—the stated rate less the 15 percent commission. As you can see, this means that the agency doesn't have to wait for publications to remit a commission, as would have to be done if the gross amount were paid. This is a strong benefit in terms of cash flow for the independent agency as well as for the house agency. Once you reach agreement with the publications you are going to use, it's simply a matter of writing net amount checks for the space used. This subject is examined in detail in Chapter 7.

Most media refuse to grant a discount to an advertiser that doesn't use an agency because they would breach the lowest rate clause with regard to other advertisers. And there are no customs or trade practices that entitle an advertiser to a deduction equal to the commissions that would have been granted to an advertising agency, if such an agency had handled the negotiations.

There's another very practical reason the media take this stance. By granting commissions directly to advertisers, they would discourage the use of advertising agencies. Not that most publications give a damn one way or another whether ad agencies survive; they just feel that they would have to take over much of the work done for them by the agencies. As you can see, there is a lot of inertia that keeps the 15 percent commission and agency recognition mentality going.

The in-house agency gives the media a legitimate reason for granting the commission, but if the in-house shop does nothing more than send insertion orders, the individual medium has the right to deny commissions. However, few people take this route when they open an in-house agency. For the most part, they are really interested in better control in a more economical fashion.

## DEALING WITH COLLATERAL SERVICES

Space advertising is only one part of the work done by an agency, whether it's in-house or independent. Those who run agencies deal with typesetters, printers, photographers, artists, writers, market researchers, and a host of other marketing and communications professionals. What are the problems that you might encounter working with these people and organizations?

Actually, you should have no problems at all. The main stumbling block to the establishment of a house agency is the media recognition factor, which I have already laid to rest. None of the other suppliers are under any pressure to grant discounts. Their prices are quoted pretty much the same for an independent agency as they are for a house agency or an advertiser that has no agency at all.

These professionals charge what they are worth—or feel they are worth. It's entirely up to you to decide whether the work they offer to do for you is worth it. One copywriter may quote $500 for the same job that another feels is worth $1,000. As I've said several times, the best price and the best service may not necessarily be the most expensive, but you can bet that the lowest price will get you in trouble every time.

Very often a free-lancer or a service company, such as a typesetter, will quote you a very low price just to get your initial business. These people then hope to recoup the loss on the first job when they bill you for later work. It may all work out, but it may not. As such people tack on little increases here and there, they often feel they can keep on going, well after they have reached the point where they have recovered the losses they had on the first job.

There is only one way to deal with suppliers, whether they are temperamental artists and copywriters, or hard-nosed printers and typesetters. Look at the work they have done for others, talk with those who have used their services, and get several competitive estimates. Once you know who can do the job, how much they have charged in the past, and how others feel about their services, you will be in the best position to make a sound judgment. But don't use differences in estimates to hassle these people into giving you lower prices. They'll make it up somewhere—they have to.

Incidentally, don't feel that just because you now have a house agency that you can't buy services from independent full-service agencies. Most agencies are more than willing to take on specific assignments on a per-job basis. Some feel that doing this may lead them into being your full-service agency when you fall on your face (they hope) and others are realistic enough to recognize that there is room enough for everyone— just as long as good work is done at fair prices.

Richard Christian, at the time he was chairman of the American Association of Advertising Agencies, was asked whether full-service agencies should accept clients on an à la carte basis. His response was: "I think that most well managed agencies, including our own [Marsteller Incorporated] should make themselves flexible enough to offer modular services, whether creative or media, or whatever, to a client. This has been going on for some time, and will continue. But agencies will always find enough clients who want the full services of a well-staffed agency."[6]

If you decide to let someone else handle your media placement, you can still use an independent agency, or one of the media buying services. I'll get into the details of these services when I talk about media in Chapter 7.

## HOW TO BE A GOOD CLIENT

If you started your house agency merely to save the commission, you'll be a rotten client. You'll treat your house agency just as you treated your advertising department, and this is the wrong way to make the concept work. When you had a department as well as an agency, the people in the ad department were, for the most part, your contact with the agency. However, now that everything is under your roof, you have to handle the situation differently.

If you have the right people, they won't let you get away with the stuff most management dumps on ad departments. Your house agency employees should be autonomous, and free from the do-this and do-that mentality that often turns very creative advertising people into gophers. They should be given the creative freedom to develop programs fully as imaginative as you could buy on the outside. The benefit of the house agency is really lost when people are dictated to. But, when they are given their head, they can often do a superior job because they are clsoer to the product, the company, and the markets than independent agency people can be. A good client is one who recognizes this and allows the house agency to go its creative way.

A good client doesn't overload the house agency with extraneous work just because it's there. In other words, don't have them turning out ads for your boat club dinner. If your independent agency was expected to do that, they should have been paid for the work. If you expect your in-house shop to do such things, expect to pay one way or another. You may end up paying by having your catalog a few days late because your in-house shop had to work on that boat club ad. There's no such thing as a free lunch, and it's nowhere more evident than in an in-house agency when every executive stakes claims on the department's time for his or her own pet projects.

I have seen very creative people leave in-house agencies because they were expected to make engineering drawings for reproduction that had formerly been bought outside when the company used an independent shop.

What I'm really saying is that you should establish some form of management by objectives for your captive shop. Determine the work that has to be done, pick the people who will do it, and set realistic goals. With this kind of thinking, there is little likelihood that you will run into the problems that have plagued many house agencies when corporate executives suddenly found that they had a new toy—an in-house advertising agency.

## Notes

[1]Robert Pulver, "Advertising Services—Make or Buy?" *Industrial Marketing*, July 1978, p. 73.

[2]Rich Young, Letter to the editor, *Industrial Marketing*, October 1978, p. 4.

[3]Gary Lewis, "In-House vs. Full Service: Why Not Consider a Consortium?" *Industrial Marketing*, June 1979, p. 68.

[4]Fred A. Tipple, "How to Manage Your Advertising," presentation, American Management Association, meeting no. 05297-50, Chicago, April 21, 1978.

[5]Robert Pulver, "Advertising Services—Make or Buy?" *Industrial Marketing*, July 1978, p. 74.

[6]Richard Christian, "Going In-House Isn't a One-Way Street," *Media Decisions*, July 1976, p. 108.

# Chapter 3

# Practical Printing and Production

When asked what portion of their budget was allocated to brochures and other printed matter, a group of house agency managers reported 37 percent. Fifty-three percent of this group also said they used outside services for the development of their sales literature.[1]

It appears that companies using house agencies depend heavily on printed promotion. It also appears that house agency people are not inclined to stick their noses into print shops. My guess is that those who have some printing experience are in the 47 percent who handle their own production. The 53 percent who buy outside help are good at something else and prefer to leave the printing projects to others.

This is more than just a guess; it's a well-educated guess. Most of those who reviewed the outline and proposal for this book said they wanted practical help to plan and buy printing. Because of this interest, I have included two chapters on printing and production.

This chapter covers the fundamentals of printing, typesetting, paper, and folding. With this information you should be able to select the right process for the printing jobs you are planning. The next chapter will help you buy printing and production services economically. Anyone can buy printing from the lowest bidder, but it takes some planning and effort to get a good price as well as a printing job you won't be embarrassed to use.

## UNDERSTANDING THE PRINTING PROCESSES

I remember reading a book on printing a number of years ago in which the author said that printing is nothing more than transferring an image from one surface to another. After this deceptive sop, he spent several hundred pages describing every detail of every printing process. At the time, I thought the author should have done a little more to ease me into his heavy material. Now I'm in the same spot, except that I have to make you printing-smart in two chapters. I suppose I can smooth my conscience by saying that none of you are planning a career in printing. But you may sink or swim with your printing as a result of what you are about to read. Therefore, may I suggest that you supplement your printing education by asking a lot of questions of a lot of printers. Some printers will be put off when you point out that the image on an offset blanket is backwards. But most realize that a knowledgeable customer is much easier to deal with. Now let's look at the printing processes that can be useful to you.

Each printing process transfers ink to paper in a different way. In order to get the best work at reasonable prices, you should understand the processes as well as the advantages and disadvantages of each. Prior to the transfer of ink to paper, however, each process requires essentially the same preparatory steps.

First there are prepress operations. These include the preparation of artwork, photographs, typography, halftones, and color separations, as well as stripping, assembly, plate-making, and press make-ready. It also includes preliminary press operations, or the work necessary to produce a proof prior to the press run.

The on-press operation is the actual transfer of ink to the paper. Some presses are fed with precut sheets of paper and others are fed from a roll called a web. When more than one color is used, it may be necessary to have a separate run for each color. However, there are presses that can print four or more colors at once. And some will print on both sides of the sheet at the same time.

Finishing operations are last: trimming, folding, die-cutting, collating, and binding.

Some presses will accept paper in one end and deliver not just a printed sheet from the other end, but a finished, bound piece. However, this equipment is most often used for long-run book and catalog manufacture.

Keep these steps in mind as you read about each of the printing processes.

## LETTERPRESS

If you have never had anything to do with printing, letterpress is the easiest process to understand. Think of an ordinary rubber stamp and the process becomes clear. The raised area on a rubber stamp, as on a letterpress plate, is inked and pressed on a piece of paper. When the plate and paper separate, an image is left on the paper. The letterpress process uses metal type and engravings made of metal or plastic to form the images. Some presses print directly from type that is held in position on the press and others make use of a plate that is made from a mold taken of the type and engravings. Good letterpress is hard to beat for quality, but the process is seldom used by industrial advertisers, unless they are running big catalogs or short runs of letterheads. The reason for this is mainly the greater flexibility of other processes such as offset. You can usually tell a letterpress job from offset by looking at the back of the sheet. Letterpress printing often creates a slight embossing of the paper. This will never occur with offset.

Modern letterpress equipment can turn out work from 1,000 to over 25,000 impressions an hour, and the presses can handle sheets ranging from post-card size to 43 x 60 inches. There are three types of letterpress, and each has certain advantages.

## Platen Press

The platen press prints from flat plates on paper that is held in position on a flat bed. Paper is fed by the sheet, either by hand or machine, to the proper position between the bed and the plate. After the type or plate has been linked by rollers, the plate is pressed against the paper and the image is transferred.

Platen presses are known in the trade as job presses, and are most often used to print short or medium runs of circulars and stationery. Because paper-cutting dies can be used with it as well as plates, the platen press is often used for die-cutting opera-

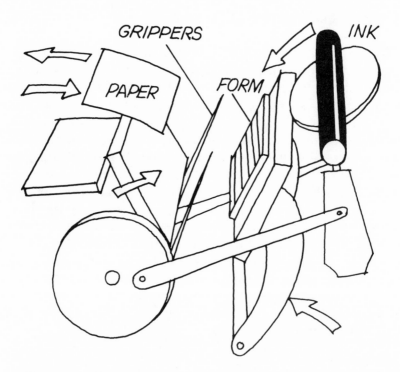

Figure 3-1  Platen press

tions. And the small job press is frequently used when printed material has to be imprinted. That is, it's used to add printing to jobs that have already been printed and folded. Manufacturers who supply catalogs to field sales offices often have the local office address added by the process of letterpress.

## Flat-bed Cylinder Letterpresses

Flat-bed cylinder letterpresses use a revolving impression drum to press a piece of paper against the inked type or plate. As the drum turns, it automatically grabs and wraps a piece of paper. The bed, on which the plate or type has been mounted, moves back and forth under the revolving cylinder. Only a small portion of the paper touches the cylinder at any given time, but

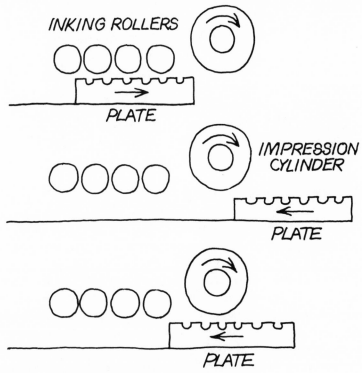

Figure 3-2   Flat-bed cylinder letterpress

when one cycle has been completed, the entire image will have been transferred to the paper. After the impression cycle, the sheet is picked off the drum, and the bed returns to its original position, ready for the next cycle. The drum has two sides. One side has a larger radius that is used to press the paper against the type. The other side has a smaller radius to allow the bed to pass under it without printing and back to the starting position.

There are a number of variations on the cylinder letterpress theme, but you won't need to know very much about any of them except, perhaps, for the perfecting flat-bed press, which prints both sides of the paper in a single operation. If your job is big enough, this type of press allows you to do a two-color, two-side job with only two passes at the press rather than the four that would be needed with a conventional press.

Flat-bed cylinder presses are most often used for printing booklets, brochures, catalogs, and packages. Single-color cylinder presses can handle sheets as large as 42 x 56 inches, and some can turn out as many as 5,000 impressions per hour. They can be used for most types of printing, ranging from work on coarse paper to fine halftone and process-color reproduction on coated paper.

The bed of a flat-bed cylinder press must return to the start position after each impression (a time-consuming step), so the press is only printing part of the total operating time.

## Rotary Letterpress

The rotary letterpress solves the problem of wasted movement by using a drum on which a curved impression plate is mounted, and a curved cylinder against which the plate prints. This press is not unlike the wringers found in a bathhouse to squeeze the water out of swimming gear. Rotary presses can be sheet-fed, or they can be supplied by a continuous web of paper. In fact, some web presses have a device called a flying paster that joins the end of one web with the start of another so the press doesn't have to shut down for web replacement. Imagine this taking place at 5,000 impressions per hour! These presses are

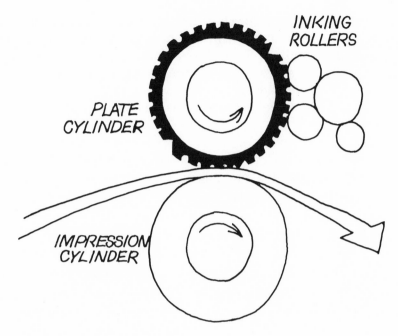

INKING
ROLLERS

PLATE
CYLINDER

IMPRESSION
CYLINDER

Figure 3-3    Rotary letterpress

usually found in newspaper plants where millions of impressions must be made daily. Web-fed presses are fitted with cutting equipment after the impression cycle so that the finished job is in sheets, not another roll of paper. Sheet-fed rotaries can handle paper as large as 54½ x 76 inches and some can turn out 6,000 impressions an hour.

While really big rotaries are used mainly for newspaper and magazine work, there are printers with smaller equipment who use it for catalogs, books, and other large assignments. Rotaries feature a higher output per hour, but the quality is not that of sheet-fed printing.

Copy can be prepared for letterpress printing several ways. The same art used to prepare work for offset can be used. That is, when art is prepared as a camera-ready mechanical, it can be used to make either a letterpress or an offset plate. There are different requirements for the preparation of halftones (photographs, or art with shading or tone) for each process. The process is described later in the chapter. However, most letterpress work that is done these days for short-run printing is printed directly from type that has been set by a Linotype, or one of the other type-casting machines. This type is locked up in a form and, when inked, pressed directly on the paper. Or, the presses are used simply to score and die-cut the work done on other presses.

Here are some highlights to consider when you're thinking of using letterpress.

1. Letterpress is direct-impression printing; the type and other material is pressed on the paper.

2. Anything that can be printed by any other process can be printed by letterpress, as long as the plates are prepared properly. It's especially important to determine which process will be used before any halftones are made.

3. Duplicate plates can be made for work that is to be done at several distant locations. However, due to their weight, it's more costly to ship letterpress plates than to send offset negatives.

4. Letterpress engravings are costly to make. If they are to be used for very long runs, they should be specially surfaced to extend their life.

5. When the piece requires only type, corrections can be made easily. It's usually just a matter of making the change on a slug of linotype metal and replacing it in the form. Changes in engraved plates and duplicates can be made, but this can be expensive.

6. Make-ready, or all the prepress steps done by the press people, can be expensive and time-consuming. However, the precision of letterpress make-ready gives the operator good control over the final presswork.

7. Proofs are relatively easy and inexpensive to get with the letterpress process. There are special proof presses, and even proving on some production presses is not especially difficult.

8. Letterpress was once the favored process for jobs that were revised regularly such as catalogs and directories.

The old type was left standing until revisions were needed and the changes were made inexpensively. However, this is no longer the case. The cost just to store the metal can be prohibitive. More important, the new electronic data-base systems have all but eliminated any of the advantages to stored metal.

## LITHOGRAPHY

Unlike the letterpress printing plate on which the image is physically higher than the areas that don't print, the printing image on a lithographic plate is at the same height as the surrounding material. Lithographic plates are called planographic plates—plates on which all areas are in the same plane. How then does an image separate itself from the background when a lithographic plate contacts the paper?

The lithographic plate is photochemically sensitive, much the same as a sheet of photographic paper. After being exposed to the light and dark variations that make up the image on the artwork that is to be printed, it is chemically processed so that only the area that is to print will have an affinity for ink. The lithographic press uses both water and ink, and the area of the plate that accepts water will not accept ink. The plate revolves through a water trough before it is inked, and because water and ink don't mix, only the area that is to print will be inked. This is the image that will print.

It is possible to print directly on paper from a lithographic plate, but this isn't done on commercial presses. The inked image is printed, or offset, on a second roller, which has been covered with a rubber blanket. The image that has been offset to this roller is then transferred to the paper. There are larger presses in which the image is transferred to other rollers, but for our purposes, it's not necessary to go into all of the variations of lithographic equipment.

Unlike letterpress, which actually presses the inked image onto a sheet of paper, an offset press just deposits the image. No squeezing takes place, as it does in a letterpress. Because of the

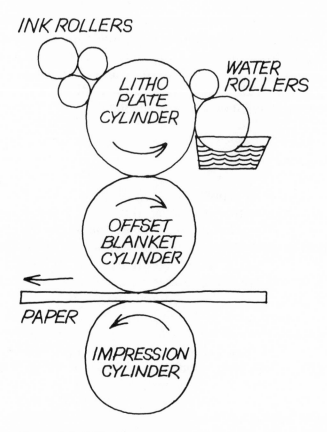

**Figure 3-4   Offset press**

flexibility of the offset roller and the way the image is transferred, it's possible to print on everything from rough, textured sheets to smooth, glossy paper. This is especially important when fine-screen halftones must be printed on rough-surfaced paper. However, only paper treated especially for offset can be used.

Most of the printing you will buy as an industrial advertiser will probably be printed on a sheet-fed offset press. Different types of sheet-fed presses are in operation with wide-ranging capabilities. Such equipment ranges from the ubiquitous Multi-lith, which is used mainly for simple duplication work to perfecting presses for multicolor work that can print paper on both sides in one operation. Most sheet-fed presses are capable of 8,000 to 10,000 impressions per hour, and some can take stock as large as 47½ x 72 inches.

For long runs, the flexibility and advantages of offset lithography are available in a number of web presses. These presses can handle webs from 17 to 76 inches wide and some can turn out work at the rate of 40,000 to 50,000 impressions an hour. If you have a large process-color catalog and require large quantities, the job will probably be done on a web offset press.

Web presses cut the sheet as it emerges from the impression area of the press and stack the printed paper ready for finishing operations. However, those with large web equipment usually automate so that the trimmed sheets are fed directly into collating, trimming, folding, and binding equipment.

Copy for offset reproduction is prepared in the form of a mechanical. When everything is in place ready for the offset cameraperson to make the negative that will be used to make the plate, the art is called camera-ready. Everything that has no tone or shading is called line work. This includes type, rules, and line drawings. Photographs are reproduced, whether by offset or letterpress, by creating an image of the picture that has been broken up by tiny dots. For mechanicals that can be converted to plates in one step, photographs are turned into halftone photographic prints called Veloxes on which the dot pattern has been interposed. When these screened prints are pasted down with all of the other line work, only one shot is needed to make the offset negative. However, halftones may also be shot separately and assembled by hand into a composite negative. This process is called stripping. When the utmost detail is required, very fine-screen halftones must be made.

Here are some points to consider when you evaluate offset lithography.

1. Offset is a rotary process, therefore it will always be faster than flat-bed letterpress.

2. Remember that an offset plate is right-reading, unlike a letterpress plate, which is backward. The offset plate transfers the image to a roller; it is then backward. The

roller then reverses the image again as it is transferred to the paper.

3. Because the image is not pressed onto the sheet, offset can be used on rough surfaces as well as smooth, and will assure good reproduction of fine-screen halftones.

4. Offset plates are made by exposing a negative on a photosensitized metal or paper plate, using a high intensity light. The negative is placed between the plate and the light to create the image. A chemical process is used to "develop" the plate.

5. Offset litho plates are thin, in one piece, and easy and relatively inexpensive to make. If changes must be made, rarely can they be made on the plate. New plates must be produced after the changes have been made on the artwork.

6. To insure quality reproduction, it's best not to make line positives that are pasted on the art. Instead, have the halftones shot separately, using finer screens, and then have them stripped into the negatives before the plates are made.

7. It's often possible to take single-color sheets that have been printed either by offset or letterpress and copy them for offset reproduction. If the work you are copying is sharp, and the halftone dots are clear and not squeezed, it's just a matter of having your offset printer use the sheet as art to make a direct line shot. Use a magnifying glass to scan the dots in the halftones to see that the edges are sharp, and to make sure that there is little fill-in.

8. If you have a long press run planned, ask the printer to make a deep-etch plate, rather than a standard offset plate. This not only saves the cost of a new plate if the first fails, it eliminates downtime and additional make-ready charges.

9. Offset proofs are made as blueprints. When the job is to be run as a single color, the blue image will be of one

tonal value. However, to show how a multiple color job will look, a composite blueprint is made, showing each color in a different value of blue. These proofs give no idea of the quality of the presswork to come, and it's difficult to determine the quality of a halftone screen from a blueprint. But they will show you in mono-chrome roughly how the finished job will appear. The best you can do is check the position of copy, pictures, and other elements, and be sure that everything registers correctly. Also check for hickies—white dots in the image area that indicate either faulty plates, lint, or inking problems.

10. Make-ready is relatively easy on an offset press, even those printing four and six colors. However, unlike letterpress where individual elements can be shifted if printing is being done with locked up individual elements, nothing but the plate itself can be shifted during offset make-ready.

11. Because they are relatively inexpensive, offset plates are seldom stored for any length of time. The plates can oxidize over time and cause problems. However, the negatives can be stored indefinitely, and it's best to use them to make new plates when a rerun is needed rather than use a stored plate that may have pitted.

## OTHER PRINTING PROCESSES

There are several other ways of getting your message on paper and each has benefits and limitations. You should know enough about them to make a choice, but you needn't under-stand the processes in any detail.

### Gravure

Think about letterpress for a moment. The ink is transferred from a raised surface to the paper. The opposite is true of gravure. The relief areas are filled with ink, and the raised areas

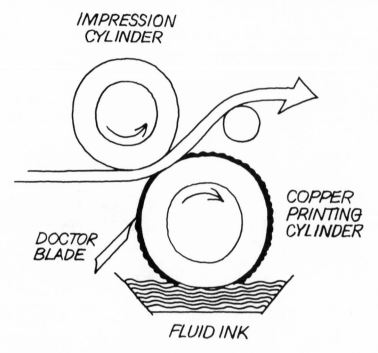

IMPRESSION
CYLINDER

COPPER
PRINTING
CYLINDER

DOCTOR
BLADE

FLUID INK

**Figure 3-5   Gravure press**

wiped clean. The process is excellent for reproducing color photographs. When speed, high quality, and a long run are important, gravure is often the best choice. However, you can lose the advantage of the process, even in large runs, if you use it only for line work. Gravure is used mainly for catalogs, newspaper supplements, and similar work. Because the equipment is large and expensive, it's seldom found in anything but large commercial printing plants. When a project calls for gravure, your printer may "job" it to a gravure printer, with your permission, of course.

Gravure paper is relatively inexpensive, therefore the cost of a long run may not be as high as it would be with other processes. However, if you're considering gravure, get an estimate for the same job done by offset.

## Screen Printing

Screen printing is used mainly by advertisers for special effects. The process is widely used to produce artistic work, but when used commercially it is mainly for posters, broadsides, and promotional pieces where a posterization effect is sought. It's possible to reproduce photographs by halftone screens, but the limitations of this work make other processes a better choice.

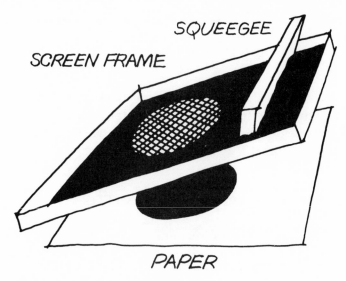

**Figure 3-6 Screen printing**

A screen, silk or other material, is prepared either photo-chemically or by hand so that the image areas that are to print are exposed to the screen. The nonprinting areas are blocked out to prevent ink from passing through. When the screen is positioned against a sheet of paper, and ink is forced through the exposed screen areas with a rubber blade squeegee, the image is transferred to the paper. The process can be done by hand, or by automated equipment. Screen printing can be used to produce single or multicolor images. It's an ideal medium for dramatic short-run work. Virtually any surface can be printed using the screen process, including those with compound shapes.

## Thermography

Most of the raised printing done today is by the thermo-graphic process. It's faster and much less expensive than steel-die engraving, which actually embosses, or raises the paper under the printed image. The thermographic process uses an ink and powder combination that is heated after printing. The heat causes the ink to expand and set hard, leaving the raised effect associated with steel-die engraving. Done well, it's impressive, but the raised ink can flake off when scratched.

## Flexography

This process, used mainly for packaging, prints with a rubber plate in the same manner as metal-plate rotary letterpress. It's best used for line work, although coarse-screen halftone work can be reproduced.

## HOW PHOTOGRAPHS ARE PRINTED

Photographic paper responds to different values of light proportionately. That is, when less light is transmitted from a negative to the photographic paper, less of the photosensitive silver particles in the paper will be developed. Hence, a photograph has continuous tone—values ranging from pure white to pure black. However, the same process cannot be used to reproduce a photograph by any of the printing processes.

To print photographs with a printing press, a process that depends on an optical illusion is used. Envision a photographic negative being used to transmit light to a metal plate that has been photochemically sensitized to react in much the same way as photographic paper. However, a screen is placed between the negative and the surface of the plate. When the image has been exposed and the plate developed, the image of the photograph will be on the plate, but it will be broken up by tiny dots. When the nonprinting area around the dots is etched away in the platemaking process, only the dots are left to print.

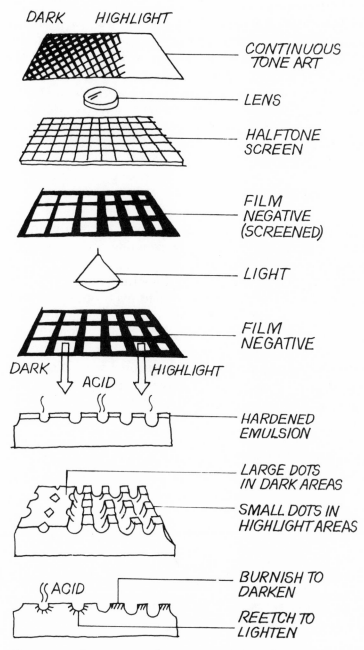

Figure 3-7  Steps required to create a halftone plate

The image is created by the dots. Each is uniformly spaced from the other, but depending on the values in the original picture, the dots will be larger or smaller. The dots are "blended" in the eye of the viewer to provide a faithful reproduction of a continuous-tone photograph.

Depending on the quality of the paper used, and the need for detail, halftones can be made with screens ranging from 55 lines per inch to 300. Screens with 120 or 133 lines per inch are most commonly used for offset.

## COLOR PRINTING

When true color is to be reproduced, individual filtered negatives are made of the art to separate the yellow, red, blue, and black colors. These separations are used to make the four plates needed to faithfully reproduce full color. When printed in the proper sequence and relation to each other, the effect is a reproduction of the original full-color photograph. Process, or four-color printing, can be very effective. Obviously, it is more expensive than running fewer colors, but if the run is large enough, it may be printed at one time on a four-color press. Color printing used to be very expensive in short runs, but the newer presses have made shorter runs much more reasonable. If you plan to run process color work, check several printers. If one printer plans to print it on a one- or two-color press, his price will probably be higher than the price quoted by a printer with a four-color press.

## TYPOGRAPHY

Unless you're going to use the typing that comes from your typewriter, you will have type set. Typewriter type can be used for price lists and quick bulletins, but the image created by professionally set type is worth the extra money.

Until recently, type had to be set by one of the several machines that cast it in lead. This type was used to print directly, or to create a reproduction proof that was then used to make plates for other printing processes.

However, the phototypesetting equipment available now has not only made typesetting more economical, it has made a lot of type available to anyone who wants to invest in the equipment. Some advertisers and agencies have their own typesetting facilities, but for the small house agency, it's probably best to use an outside service that has the equipment and the experience. Installing typesetting equipment is not unlike adding production equipment to your plant. If you can justify it economically, do it. However, I think too many people feel they can make do with untrained people to run the typesetting equipment in their spare time. Whichever way you go, you should know something about type, and here's the short course.

There are literally thousands of typefaces. Each falls into one of these general classifications:

*Oldstyle* Based on classic Roman inscriptions, this face has smooth, rounded serifs (embellishments at the ends of the letters).

*Transitional* There is a greater contrast between thicks and thins in this style.

*Modern* Note the big contrast between thicks and thins, and the lack of roundness in the serifs.

*Sans serif and gothic* Faces in this family have no serifs.

*Square serif* This face is characterized by its square, block serifs.

*Script* Faces in this style are attempts to create the look of handwriting. Some are quite elegant, others are loose and casual.

*Novelty and ornamental* These faces were created to convey very special images.

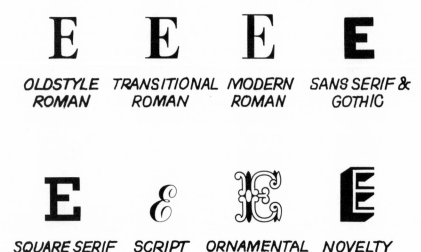

OLDSTYLE  TRANSITIONAL  MODERN  SANS SERIF &
ROMAN        ROMAN        ROMAN        GOTHIC

SQUARE SERIF   SCRIPT   ORNAMENTAL   NOVELTY

Figure 3-8   Typeface styles

When a letter is vertical with respect to the line on which it is printed, it is said to be roman (not to be confused with the typeface called Roman). Type positioned at an angle to the line is italic. Typefaces can vary from very light to very bold. They can be condensed or expanded. When you think of these variations in terms of the thousands of faces that are available, you can see that the number of choices is boggling. However, unless you are seeking special effects, you will probably stick to faces in the transitional or sans serif style, and play with the weight and posture variations to give you the effects you need.

Designing with type is not as easy as it seems. Too many amateurs try to attract attention by using wild combinations of faces. This may attract attention, but not the kind you want. Gimmickry in typography slows down reading and the comprehension of the message. Since it's impossible to condense the thousands of pages that have been written by others on the subject of typographic design, let me give you just a few points that will, at least, keep you out of trouble.

1. Limit your type selection to as few faces as possible. If possible, use one face in different sizes and weights to create the visual effects you want.

2. When you use more than one face, make sure they are compatible. For example, an old style and a modern Roman face would probably not look well together. But a clean sans serif used with either the old style or the modern would probably work out. Try for bolder sans serif faces in headlines and use medium-weight faces with serifs for the text.

3. Avoid using capitalized or boldface words within the text. Many people think that such emphasis helps to make a point, but it really makes it more difficult to read. Make your point with well-written prose, not with typographical gimmicks.

4. Try for a few points of leading space between your text lines. A point is 1/72 of an inch, the standard unit used to measure type and the spacing between it. A point or two between lines can lighten the overall appearance of the block of copy and make it easier to read.

5. Much industrial literature and advertising copy can be improved by using ragged lines either right, left, or both, rather than setting the text in a square block. Have the type set to conform to the design of the ad, rather than plopping down a block of text. Rectangles are predictable and uninteresting.

6. The type you select must fit in the area indicated on the layout. In order to do this, you will need samples of the type you will use. Count the number of characters in the typewritten manuscript including punctuation and spaces between words. Then count the number of characters in the type style you have chosen that will fit in the line length on the layout. Divide the former by the latter and you will have the total number of lines that the typesetting will occupy. For example:

    a. A manuscript of 750 characters.

    b. 8-point Century Bold (the type selected) will have 69 characters in the 3-inch line width shown on the layout.

    c. 750 divided by 69 yields 11 lines of 8-point type—the depth of the setting. A block of type 88 points high is just a little over one inch deep. Remember that there are 72 points to the inch. If you want the type to fill more area, spacing between the lines can be added. This is called leading.

7. Unless you are an artist, it doesn't pay to try to be a typographic designer when doing your own sales literature. Turning an amateur loose in a type shop is like giving a baby several cans of paint and a nice white wall. The best advice I can give you is to rely on a typesetter or a free-lance artist to help you with the design aspects of your printing. Of course, if you're going to set up a full-fledged house agency, you will have a commercial artist on staff.

8. Buying type requires a little shopping. There is a lot of competition, not only between those with metal (hot) and photographic (cold) typesetting systems, but between those using the same systems. Get competitive estimates from several sources, giving each typesetter exactly the same specifications on which to quote. Check delivery times and look carefully at the quality of the samples shown to you. Some Linotype faces are abused and you will be able to spot cracks and hairlines on the sample work. Some phototypesetters are sloppy in their work and the edges of the type may not be especially sharp. The best way for the uninitiated to get a feel for quality is to look at all of the samples at the same time, and to use a powerful magnifying glass. To reproduce well, all edges of type should be sharp, clean, and distinct. Look for alignment, proper spacing, and evenness of the total typographic image.

9. Type is set to your specifications. If you make any errors, the typesetter will make the changes but you will be charged for them as author's alterations. Watch your work carefully before it goes to the typesetter and you will have few AA's.

## HOW TO SELECT AND BUY PAPER

The choice of paper has as much to do with the appearance of the final job as the design, type, and artwork. Paper should be chosen not only for its esthetic contribution, but for its compatability with the printing process being used. These are the papers you are most likely to encounter when you plan and buy your own printing:

*Coated* The smooth and glossy papers are specially finished with coatings made of clay derivitives or plastic compounds. These sheets run from dull to very glossy sheets. Coated papers provide excellent quality reproduction, but very glossy sheets will reflect light much like a mirror, interfering with reading.

*Book* Made mainly for use in book manufacture, as the name implies, these papers are available from fairly coarse English (rough) surfaces to supercalendered (smooth) sheets. They are less expensive than text papers and are available in a wide range of weights.

*Text* Noted mainly for the variety of colors and textures in which they are made, text papers are most effective when used to print type and line art by letterpress.

*Offset* Offset paper is specially treated to resist the water that is used in offset presses. Most offset papers can be used with other presses, but most other papers must be treated before they can be used on an offset press.

*Cover* Cover stock is made in heavier weights than other papers. As its name implies, it is most often used to make a cover for pieces printed on lighter-weight paper. It's available in a wide range of surfaces, colors, weights, coatings, and finishes.

*Bond* Used mainly for stationery, bond paper is made to accept typewriter ink readily, yet be erasable. The better bonds have a high cotton-fiber content.

Many other types of paper are made, but the papers just described are the most useful for the industrial advertiser. You may need very stiff paper for boxes and displays, or a sheet made specifically for a label. When these needs arise, it's best to plan carefully with your printer, rather than try to second-guess him on the right stock to use.

The standard unit of paper is the ream, and one ream is 500 sheets. However, you must know the basis size in order to determine the weight, which is the standard measure used to sell paper. The basis size is the size in inches in which a particular paper is most commonly produced. The basis weight in pounds is based on the weight of one ream of paper and its basis size. Thus, the basis size of book paper is designated as 25 x 38 basis 70. This means that one ream of this paper this size weighs 70 pounds. The stock is commonly called a 70-pound sheet, even when sold in different size sheets.

Here are some tips to help you select and buy paper:

1. You can save money by buying paper directly from a paper house and having it shipped to the printer. But, unless you know your stuff and plan to buy a lot of paper, you are generally better off having the printer buy the paper for you.

2. The paper should be picked to meet the criteria of the job. Consider strength, durability, foldability, and permanence. If you're going to print on both sides, be sure that the paper has sufficient opacity to prevent the impressions from showing through.

3. Be sure that the paper you select can be used by the printing process you have chosen.

4. Be sure that the quality of the paper matches the intended use of the piece. If you're reproducing four-color photographs, a quality sheet will be needed. Price lists that become obsolete quickly can be done on a much less expensive paper.

5. Select the weight of the paper carefully. Choose a heavier weight if the piece is to last and have a lot of use. Many lightweight but durable stocks are available when mailing costs are important.

6. Choose the surface of the paper not only to be compatible with the printing process selected, but to reproduce the image well. Halftones reproduce better on smooth sheets, but the soft effect of an antique finish may be just what is needed for the overall image of the piece.

7. Paper should be bought in sizes from which the most economical cuts can be made. Many jobs are printed on the finished size, such as an 8½ x 11 inch flyer, but larger jobs are often run on big presses on which many impressions are ganged on a single sheet. When the job has to be cut from a larger sheet, and there is waste stock, it will be expensive. However, the planning for this should take place long before any paper is bought. Your designer and your printer should work together to make sure that the job can be printed from a standard sheet with a minimum of waste.

8. Not all white paper is white—pure white, that is. At random, take any ten different pieces of product literature from your file and compare the whiteness. Some are grey, others tinged with color. The point is this: Don't just say white, pick the white you want from a printer's stock book.

9. If you're going to use a colored stock, make sure that the color is compatible with the image to be printed on the sheet. It's a little disconcerting to see a person's face printed on a blue sheet. Try a paper with colors that range toward the warm skin tones and you'll be safe.

## TRIMMING AND FOLDING

Unless you're printing flyers on an 8½ x 11 inch sheet, your job will probably require some trimming. The cutting work is done in a power guillotine, and you needn't concern yourself with the details, except to make sure that the most economical size sheet was used to begin with.

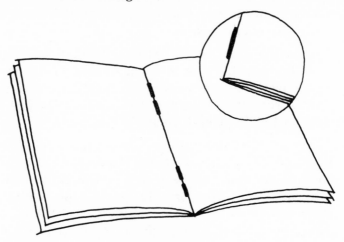

**Figure 3-9    Saddle-stitch binding**

Most advertising brochures that exceed four pages are saddle-stitched. That is, staples are used on the crease to hold the folded sections together. Larger catalogs can be bound in the same manner as books, or they can be assembled using one of the many types of plastic-comb binding systems. The plastic comb system requires special punching as well as an assembly device to insert the comb in the punched sheets. If you go the comb route, you gain some flexibility when you do not bind all your catalogs at once. If your line changes, you may want to add or remove pages, and the plastic-comb method allows you to do this. Collated sheets are kept unbound, and pages can be substituted whenever assembled catalogs are needed.

If you think that all sales literature has to be 8½ x 11 inches and folded just one way, take a look at some of these folds. All can be done with ordinary folding equipment, and depending on

your designs, will add an interesting touch to your sales
literature.

Figure 3-10   Some folding ideas

## Notes

[1]Rick Braithwaite, "Investigation into the In-House versus Full-Service Advertising
Agency Situation in the United States," unpublished report, California State University,
Fullerton, 1977, p. 20.

# Chapter 4

# How to Save Money on All the Printing You Buy

Printers are no different from the rest of us—they're in business to make money. But, to listen to some advertisers, you'd think that all printers overcharge and hide behind a language known only to those with inky fingers. The truth is that there are so many printers competing for business that few of them are willing to take a chance with an inflated price, even when the customer appears to know little or nothing about printing.

I've found that most of the misunderstandings between advertisers and printers result from not knowing the customs of the industry. For example, many who have never bought printing think they are being robbed when they place an order six months after being given a quotation, and find themselves billed a higher price. Printing quotations are given for specified time periods. As inflation eats further into the economy, the quotation periods have become shorter and shorter. To prevent this problem, be sure to check the date on the quotation before you place an order. If you place an order after the quotation period elapses, ask for an updated figure. However, if you place an order within the period and are billed for more than the quotation, complain.

Let's look at some of the other trade customs before we get into the practical ways to keep your bills low and the printing quality high.

*Condition of copy* The condition of the material you give a printer has a lot to do with the price you will be charged. If you have clean, professionally prepared mechanicals that are ready for the camera, the price will be less than if the printer has to strip, paste up, clean up, and make corrections. This, incidentally, is a good reason to use a professional artist or an agency to prepare your work. You will have to pay the artist, but his or her work will probably save you quite a bit on the printing bill. And, of course, it will be a professional job.

*Ownership of preparatory materials* Any work created by the printer, such as copy, sketches, or dummies, is his exclusive property unless you have agreed to pay for it. (Of course, artwork commissioned by you from an independent artist or agency is your property.) Plates, negatives, positives, and other materials used in the printing processes are the property of the printer. Don't ask a printer, or anyone else for that matter, to do work for you on speculation and expect to own it if you decide not to use it. If you have given a printer an assignment, and all prep work has been finished, including stripping, negatives, and plates, expect to be billed for the work, even if the job isn't printed.

If you find another printer willing to reprint a job for less than you were charged by the original printer, the original printer is under no obligation to give you the plates or negatives, although he may be willing to sell them to you. It is possible to write a clause into your agreement with a printer that makes the plates your property. But, in the absence of an agreement, you have no right to the material.

*Experimental work* If you ask a printer to make a test run or do any graphic development work, expect to be billed for the time and materials at prevailing rates.

*Proofs* Check your proofs carefully. Most printers will not run a job unless the proof has been returned with an "OK," or an "OK with corrections." If you find an error after the job has been printed and you have approved the proof, you have no recourse. Your OK absolves the printer, so read proof carefully before signing it away. Most printers won't accept a verbal release. But if one does, and there is a problem, it will probably land in your back yard.

*Alterations* Changes, other than those made to correct a printer's goof, are charged at current rates. These author's alterations (AA's) can be expensive. If you plan your job carefully, and make sure the copy you give the printer is perfect, you'll have few problems.

*Order cancellation* Once you place an order, it can't be cancelled without compensating the printer for losses that he or she may sustain. Even though the printer may not have gotten to making the plates when the order was cancelled, the cost of cancellation may still be high. Printers buy paper early so it will be in the shop and ready to run when they have finished their prep work. Unless the paper house is willing to take it back, or the printer can use it for another job, you will probably have to pay for the paper.

*Overruns and underruns* There is always some loss in a print run. Make-ready uses paper, and press adjustments during the run account for further losses. For this reason, printers order additional stock for each job. If they are lucky, they will hit the quantity on the nose. If they are very lucky, there may be more than the quantity ordered by the customer. When this happens, or when fewer pieces are shipped, you will be charged accordingly. Standard terms state that overruns or underrruns not to exceed 10 percent of the amount ordered will constitute an acceptable delivery and the excess or deficiency will be charged or credited to the customer proportionately.

*Protection of customers' material* Printers are expected to carry sufficient insurance to cover all of your artwork against fire, vandalism, sprinkler leakage, and other problems. Be sure that your printer has this coverage before you agree to have him or her store your work.

These are the highlights of the printing trade customs. However, there are other points to be considered when dealing with a printer. You will want to get a firm agreement on delivery conditions. Unless otherwise specified, the price is usually quoted for a single shipment, without storage, FOB the local customer's place of business, or FOB the printer's platform for an out-of-town shipment.

Most printers' invoices are rendered net, thirty days. If you want to arrange other terms, do it before you give the go-ahead to the printer. Some printers don't mind financing work for clients, but the terms and interest, if any, should be spelled out and agreed to in advance.

Claims for defects must be made within thirty days of the acceptance of the job. Of course, you can make any other agreements you want, but in the absence of them, standard printing trade customs will prevail.

## FOURTEEN WAYS TO SAVE MONEY ON PRINTING

There's more to saving money on printing than haggling with a dozen printers over nickels and dimes. You can usually save the most money by starting out with a clear idea of the sales objectives of the piece and a professional plan to produce it. Anyone can call in a top designer, have it run on expensive paper with tricky die-cuts and mail it in a beautiful, hand-screened envelope. If it brings in the business, the effort and expense may be justified. But suppose you ran the same job on a less expensive sheet, eliminated the hand-screened envelope, and the die-cut? If the piece produced the same number of sales, the profit on the program would, obviously, be higher.

However, no one knows beforehand how far to go in either direction before the curves cross. Heavy corner-cutting can do as much to reduce profits by making the piece less effective as spending too much money on the job. The point is this: Plan your printing to do the best job without making the piece look cheap, and without spending more than you could hope to recover in sales.

Unfortunately, the choice for most industrial advertisers is seldom this clear-cut. Their choice usually involves a decision, such as whether to run the brochure in one or two colors, or whether to use a 6 x 9 inch sheet or one that measures 8½ x 11 inches. The individual cost differences are usually small, but most industrial advertising budgets are modest affairs. If enough of these pieces are planned for a year, the difference might add up to enough money for you to increase your media schedule by a few ads.

Over the years that I have been buying printing for the catalogs, mailers, brochures, and other printed pieces we create for our clients, I have found the following to be most effective in keeping printing costs in line.

1. The most comon cause of added expense is the overtime that must be paid for when alterations are made and when jobs are left until the last minute. If you plan your work well ahead of your need, you will have plenty of time to make mistakes when they won't cost you money. It doesn't cost much to make changes in typewritten copy, but it can cost a bundle to reset type and make new printing plates when errors are discovered. If you get to the blueprint proof stage and find a mistake, or decide to make changes for other reasons, all of the savings you made by haggling over the lowest price may be lost. Be sure to allow enough time for everyone at each step to do an unhurried job. Take a page from the printer's book: Start with the date you need the finished piece and work backward, plugging in dates in a working schedule when each step should be completed.

2. If you're going to do your own layout, make sure it's clear and accurate before you hand it over to the printer. Don't just draw a circle to show the printer where the pictures and copy go. Be sure that everything fits. If you have any doubt, have the layout done by a professional.

3. Apart from the obvious problems you can have if you have no artistic training and are designing your own printing, the problems you will have when you get to the point of printing will be something else. Commercial artists are trained in printing production and can show you how to get what you want in a design that can be run economically. When the printer and the artist work together, they can plan the best way to run the job.

Often minor changes in the art can save you considerable amounts of money.

4. Check the artwork carefully before it goes to the printer. If there are any errors on the art, they should be corrected before negatives and plates are made. If there is a chance that something will be changed, such as prices and specifications, hold up on everything until you are sure that the information is firm. You'd be surprised at how much is spent at this level that needn't be.

5. Small differences in the size of a printed piece seldom make much difference in the total impact, unless you are going to cram a lot of material into a smaller format. In this case, it's false economy to use a smaller sheet. As long as the information you want to include is clear, easy to read, and presented in a professional way, the smaller sheet probably won't account for any loss in business compared with the results you might have gotten with a larger sheet run at greater expense.

6. Stick to standard paper sizes. You may have a super idea but find that it cuts uneconomically, leaving a lot of waste paper. If the job justifies the expense, do it. But most jobs can be planned for standard paper sizes for less money.

7. Don't waste your money on a glossy sheet unless you are running quality process color. Glossy stock is very expensive and it should be varnished to protect the printed image. Varnishing requires another pass at the press that must be paid for. Glossy paper reflects considerable light, and the feeling of quality it engenders is often lost by the difficulty people can have reading the message on it.

8. If the job calls for folding, make sure that the paper you select can be folded. The heavier the stock, the more difficult it is to fold. You may find that the paper will crack, and if there is important copy at the fold, your

message may be lost. Heavy paper can be folded, but it is usually scored on a letterpress first. This, of course, is another step that adds to the cost.

9. Paper has grain. Make sure that your printer knows which way the job is to be folded so he can print the sheet appropriately. A sheet folded against the grain can crack and look awful.

10. Ask your printer to look into job-lot paper. It's often possible to buy good sheets at great savings. But remember that you may not be able to match the stock if you have to rerun the job in the future.

11. Avoid three-color printing. Web presses do exist that can print three colors on one side and one on another at one pass, but they are not common, and are uneconomical for smaller runs. Two- and four-color presses are much more common, and most people feel that two-color jobs are more cost effective than three-color jobs.

12. If you have a short, two-color run, get estimates from printers with small, single-color presses. They can often be less expensive, running one color at a time than a printer who would run two colors at once on a larger press. Large web presses should only be considered for long runs.

13. If you are running two jobs that can be ganged on one press, you will save money. And you can get each job in a different color, even though you are using a single-color press. This printing magic is done with a split fountain. An offset press feeds ink to its rollers from a trough called a fountain. When the job is planned so each piece can be separated from the other vertically with respect to the image blanket, it's possible to split the fountain and fill each section with a different color ink, but there will be no extra charge for paper. Only one plate will be used, and everything will be handled in a single press run. You will eliminate two press wash-ups, two make-ready steps, and two press runs. The one

make-ready will take a little more time than would a single-color set-up, but the additional cost will be more than offset by the economy of a single press run.

14. Don't approve anything unless it's correct and you know exactly what the result will be.

## HOW TO SELECT A PRINTER

Before you choose a printer, you must determine the process that will be best for the work you are planning. That's what the previous chapter was all about. Some printers have letterpress as well as offset equipment, but you are more likely to find printers working with either one process or the other. Most industrial advertisers use offset for the bulk of their work, leaving letterpress for imprinting material that has already been printed, and for die-cutting. In the case of the latter, the work will probably be jobbed out—given to the appropriate letterpress printer by the firm that does your offset work. You can save some money by contracting separately for each process yourself, but the time it takes to coordinate everything is seldom worth it when you have more important things to do. It's generally best to leave all of the details up to one printer—your general contractor—but make sure that all costs are spelled out separately. If you ever run the job again, and do it with another printer, you should know the cost of each step in order to evaluate the new price.

It's best to get a clear picture of just which operations are handled in-house by the printer you select and which will be farmed out. There is really nothing wrong with one printer jobbing work to another, as long as the prime contractor assumes full responsibility for the job, and as long as it's done with your consent.

This may seem silly, but in some regions of the country you should be sure that the printers you use have climate-controlled shops: You want to know that your work will dry quickly after it has been printed. Printed sheets must be dry before they are trimmed, folded, or run through the press again for addtional impressions. If you live in a high-humidity region, it could take

days between impressions before your work is dry enough to use
or continue processing. You might also ask if the presses are
equipped with heat or powdering devices that speed up the
drying process.

Be sure that the printer you choose does a lot of the type of
work you are planning to buy. The printer may have the presses
and equipment needed to produce the job, but if it is seldom
used, the quality of the job may not be up to par. For example,
printers who specialize in book work often have small offset
presses to handle an occasional insert or mailing piece for their
publisher clients. However, their strength is in big press work.
Such printers would probably not do much short-run work, and
your job could suffer with one of them. You can solve the
problem, regardless of how often the printer tells you he runs the
press, by asking for a number of recent samples run on the press.

Look carefully at the work that is being turned out on the
press that will be used for your job. Check the halftones to make
sure they are sharp and clear. Use a magnifying glass to look at
the dot structure to determine if the edges are sharp. Look at jobs
that have been run on the press that have large areas of ink
coverage. If the coverage is uneven, it could be because the job
was run on the wrong press or it could be sloppy workmanship.
Most Multilith presses are not capable of heavy ink coverage
over large areas. If your job calls for heavy inking, ask the printer
to use a press with the appropriate inking capability.

Look at registration—the point where two or more colors or
line work join. Unless the art was prepared to overlap, you can
spot sloppy work here, too.

Most printers provide faster and less expensive service to
regular customers once they have become accustomed to their
working habits. Don't underestimate this benefit. If you are like
most other industrial advertisers, you will probably leave your
printing until the last minute. A printer who has worked with
you will be more inclined to help you than one who finds
himself handed a rush job as his first assignment.

Not every printer is in business to turn out top quality work.
Although there are some who will try to assure you that their
work is tops, no matter how bad it looks, there are those for

whom a large volume of less critical work is more important than a smaller volume of quality printing. These printers are usually honest about their standards. They are the printers who run price lists, sales letters, simple brochures, and folders. Don't give such a printer your elaborate color work and expect to get quality work. And, it can often be a mistake to allow such a printer to job the work to another printer who has the equipment and people to handle the job. The printer who does the jobbing must take full responsibility, and if his standards are not up to the work that will be done by the jobbing printer, you may not get the best quality.

Once you have selected a printer, establish the lines of communication that will exist for your work. In some shops, the salesperson, or account executive, is given full responsibility for liaison with the client. There are pitfalls in this relationship because printing salespeople are expected to sell new business while they are handling the work they have sold. If you need information in a hurry on a job that is being run at the moment, you won't want to wait until the salesperson gets back to the shop at the end of the day to return your call.

If you don't make it appear that you are slighting the salesperson, and do not take up too much of the time of the production staff in the plant, most printers will let you communicate directly with the individuals working on the different parts of your job. But don't abuse the privilege. You can learn a lot from the stripper, cameraperson, and the press operator that will make you a better customer in the future, but every print-shop owner knows that time is money. When his staff is talking with you, nothing productive will be happening with the work in the shop.

Once you have found the printer or printers who can deliver quality work at fair prices, stick with them. You should give as much thought to switching printers as you would to firing and hiring employees. Don't make them go through tough competitive bidding for every job, but never authorize a job until you have been given a quotation in writing.

Now that you know just what to look for in printers and equipment, the next step is finding enough printers to talk with so you can make an intelligent decision. You should begin with the yellow pages or your local telephone directory. Many of the printers listed in these sections tell enough about themselves in their ads so that you can add them to your list, or rule them out before you waste any time.

You will find two directories helpful as well. Both list printers, lithographers, binders, typographers, engravers, paper merchants, and manufacturers and suppliers of other graphic services. The *Printing Trade Blue Book*, one of the directories, is published in three editions: Metropolitan New York, Northeastern, and Southeastern. The *Graphic Arts Green Book* covers the Midwest. Write to A. F. Lewis & Company at 853 Broadway, New York, NY 10003 for current prices and a brochure describing the editions in which you are interested.


## HOW TO NEGOTIATE A FAIR PRICE

Printers' estimates are based on the equipment and people they have that are suitable for the job, as well as their desire to get the work and their personal standards. The lowest bidder may be willing to take the first job at a loss just to get a crack at your future business. But sooner or later the prices you pay will be adjusted to make up for the loss of profit on early work. You should be able to spot a printer who is doing this. Printers' estimates usually cluster closely, but a printer who is throwing you a low ball will be way out of line. If you really like the work done by this printer, but suspect the price is deliberately very low to get your business, be open about it. Tell him or her that you like the work being done in the shop, but want to make sure that the relationship gets off on the right foot. Most printers will welcome this frankness and will work especially hard to keep your business by offering very competitive prices.

It's a mistake to move from one printer to another, trying to save money each time with a low first-job estimate. As competitive as they are, when someone pulls a stunt like this, the printers will close ranks and spread the word quickly. You may discover the next printer you use will conveniently find excuses to hold up on your rush job—or worse.

If you find a printer whose estimate is much higher than his competitors', let him know. It's possible that he or she made a computational error. Seldom is an extremely high price a sign that a printer thinks he can retire early on the profits from your work.

When you ask for estimates, get itemized figures for each of the steps involved. Assuming that you are supplying camera-ready copy, these costs include the preparatory work of stripping, and making negatives and plates as well as the press make-ready. It isn't necessary to have all of the prep steps estimated separately. Just get an estimate that separates the prep work from the other steps and details all the items that will be part of the prep work.

In addition to costs for the preparation steps, you will need to know how much each printer plans to charge for paper, press time, and any finishing and binding that may be required. When each printer is given the same specifications and the same request for an itemized quotation, you will be in a much better position to make a good choice. And you can spot potential problems. For example, if two printers quote the same total price for a job, but you find one is higher on prep charges and the other is higher on press costs, you should look into the situation. You might find that one printer is paying less attention to the prep work, and, as a result, your job might suffer. It could also mean that the job is not being run on the appropriate press. The printer quoting more for press time may be planning to run the job on a smaller press that would require more impressions than the other press. Since press work is billed as a function of time, this printer's press estimate would be high. It could turn out that the smaller press is not capable of the quality you expect in the job. If you don't get itemized estimates, you will have no way of digging into important details.

Printing costs fall into two categories: fixed and running expenses. The fixed costs include all steps necessary to get the job on the press. If you have a job that requires elaborate printer preparatory work, but will only be a short press run, the ratio of prep work to running costs may seem way out of line. I've seen jobs for which the prep costs exceeded the running costs by quite a bit. And I've seen press runs of several hundreds of thousands that made the prep cost ratio seem very small. When getting estimates, remember that prep costs will remain fixed, regardless of how many pieces are printed.

This is not unlike situations I encounter occasionally in which the cost to prepare an ad exceeds the cost of the space in the magazine that will run it. It's not that the cost to prepare the ad is high, it's that the cost of space in the magazine is very low.

Every printer, until he or she has worked with you for a while, will have to guess at the amount of time that will be spent servicing you. It's not enough for a printer to estimate only his production, labor, and paper costs. He or she must anticipate whether you will be easy to work with, or whether you will be a time-consuming nit-picker. Sometimes they guess right and at other times they end up holding hands with nervous clients and losing money on their work. But the printer who goofs on an initial estimation will adjust his price on future work to compensate for the time that must be spent. You can save money by being a model customer. This is not to say that you should undertake any of the work the printer is expected to do, or let the printer push you around. But if you can run your jobs through the shop with a minimum of fuss, your efforts will pay off in smaller bills. However, don't take this for granted. Speak up when you know that the prices should be adjusted.

Whatever you do, don't invite two printers to the same meeting and expect them to compete in the open for your work. Meet and deal with each individually. By the same token, be absolutely open with each when asking for estimates. Be sure that each has the same specifications on which to quote.

## SHOULD YOU CONSIDER AN IN-HOUSE PRINTING PLANT?

I once considered buying a going printing plant to handle most of the work for my agency. It was tempting. I had been dealing with the printer for many years, and the owner was a top craftsman. He had good equipment, and the price was right. At the time, our volume with this printer was in excess of one hundred thousand dollars a year. Simply put, the situation had a lot going for it. But I decided against it.

I decided not to do it mainly because it would have limited the flexibility of the agency. Even though my agency bought a lot of printing from the owner of the plant, we also bought from others who had different equipment and capabilities. If we had bought the plant, I felt we would have designed our work to suit the equipment to make the most of the investment. No one needs this kind of creative constraint, especially in a business such as ours whose stock and trade is creative flexibility.

There was another reason. Even though I deal with printers every day, theirs is another world—another business. I felt that my agency would be better off sticking with the work we know and do best, even though a large part of it involves printing.

I think that you should view the idea of a captive printing plant from the same point of view. Unless you are spending millions in printing and can afford the best craftspeople and equipment, a print shop can be a compromise. However, if your work is limited to a few formats, and there is no need to change, a captive plant can be a benefit if there is sufficient volume.

Typesetting is another thing. There is such a variety of good, easy-to-use equipment available that many agencies and advertisers are now setting their own type. However, if you do it, don't do it only to save money. Unless you have a sufficient volume of typography, the equipment you install may be underutilized. If you do install typesetting equipment, the main reason should be to gain flexibility and control. You may need type faster than outside services can supply it, or you may be updating a big price list that requires new type daily. If you do save money in the bargain, consider it an added benefit.

Some people have bought typesetting equipment for their own use and ended up selling the service to others either to pay for it, or to keep the salaried operator busy. Before you consider buying any typesetting equipment, talk with others who have done it and make a careful analysis of the use that will be made of the equipment. It may work out for you, but if it doesn't, you will find yourself with an expensive, underutilized piece of equipment.

# Chapter 5

# Tested Methods for Writing Copy

Every word you write about your product should be written to sell. Don't think that just because you are writing a few paragraphs for a technical data sheet that the rules of sound copywriting don't apply. And don't think that just because your product is bought and used by intelligent, sophisticated people that they will be repelled by a sales pitch. I don't mean that all your copy should be hard sell, but I do mean that you should always think of what the prospect wants to hear and be sure that you say it. Don't waste a word. In today's visual world, people are much less accustomed to reading than they were a few years ago. So when they read anything about your product, be sure that they get the message—your message.

Writing good advertising copy involves a lot more than just choosing and arranging words. Your copy may have style and read well, but unless it has a central selling idea and talks in terms of benefits that are important to the prospect, it won't be very effective. Your copy should attract and hold attention as it turns curiosity into action. Perhaps the toughest thing for the novice copywriter to realize is that his or her writing is not an end in itself—it's a means to a sale. And it's important to recognize that copywriting is one-way communication. All questions the reader may ask should be anticipated and answered, and there should be specific directions for the reader to follow. If you want the readers to send for your catalog, say so. Don't beat around the bush.

Whether you're going to write the copy yourself, have someone in your in-house shop do it, or buy it from free-lancers, you should understand the principles of persuasive writing. If you don't know a feature from a benefit, and you insist on pushing a blue pencil all over someone's copy, you're not going to get anything but blisters on your fingers. The best advice I can give you under any circumstances is not to write a word until you know everything there is to know about the product and the people you want to buy it. The following seven questions will help put the product in focus before you attempt any writing.

## THE SEVEN KEY QUESTIONS TO ASK ABOUT THE PRODUCT

1. *What is the product made of?*
If you make your product of stainless steel and your competitors use carbon steel, yours won't rust and the competitors' will. That can be an important difference. But remember that the use of stainless is a feature; the fact that it won't rust is a benefit. Play up the benefit first, and then get into the features to tell why your product won't rust. Even if you don't have a major difference, you must be able to latch onto something that will give you a selling advantage. Those who make mixing-type faucets like to point out that their product doesn't have any washers and therefore cannot leak. It may seem like a small point, but when you can point out that highly-paid plant maintenance people spend considerable time replacing washers in conventional faucets, you will have turned a small feature into an important benefit. If you can actually show how many man-hours and how much money is saved by the switch to a mixing valve, you will have answered the question every plant manager will ask.

2. *Are construction details important?*
Most competitive products start out with essentially the same raw materials, but because of differences in design or workman-

ship, the finished products may be very different. Two manufacturers, for example, may buy the same steel from the same
foundry to make hammers, but one hammer may be much better
than the other because of a unique heat-treating step in its
manufacture. It's not enough to say that the hammer is heat-
treated, though; you have to tell the reader of your çopy that the
face won't chip because it's specially heat-treated. Always stress
benefits.

3. *What does the product do best?*
Most products have several features and benefits that will appeal
to prospects. Before you write a word, determine which of the
benefits will be most important to the largest segment of your
market and don't let the others overshadow it. Suppose you
make a voltmeter with a range from 0 to 100,000 volts. If your
market is made up of plant electricians who seldom encounter
voltages this high, but who want a meter that can be dropped
from a smokestack and still work, there is no question about
which benefit to play up. Use all the other benefits in the copy,
but only after you are sure that the main point has been made.

4. *How important are your competitive differences?*
Your product may be better than that of a competitor on a point
that doesn't make any real difference to the person who must
make the choice. Don't be fooled into using this advantage as a
benefit. If, for example, your antifreeze contains more glycol
than the antifreeze made by your competitor and sets the
temperature to $-75°F$, this is not a benefit to people who live
where the temperature seldom gets below 20°F. Just comparing
your specifications with those of your competitors is seldom
enough to do the job. You must present the differences in ways
that will help the prospects see them as beneficial. When you say
that your antifreeze contains more glycol than all the others,
your prospects may say so what. But when you say that your
antifreeze can be used on arctic expeditions, it's meaningful for
those who go on arctic expeditions.

Even if you have a great competitive advantage over other
products, don't knock the competitors. But do make sure that
your reader knows the difference and appreciates what it will
mean if your product is bought.

5. *Where and how can the product be purchased?*
Once you get people interested enough in your product to either want more information or to buy it, you will have to tell them where and how it can be bought. If you're trying to sell directly from the ad, don't mince words—tell the readers how much to send and where to send their money. If you're using salespeople, reps, or distributors, you might let them know who their local sales agent is. Don't leave anything to chance. It may seem as though "call now for information" is a blinding glimpse of the obvious, but I can assure you that few people will call unless you tell them to.

6. *Do you have a price advantage or a price problem?*
If you do not have an advantageous price, just don't say a thing about price. But you had better make sure that your benefits are strong enough to get people interested so that when you follow up directly they will be sufficiently interested to pay a higher price.

If you do have a price advantage, let your readers know. You may not want to include the actual price in the ad, but you can make many sales points just by saying that your product sells for less than the others.

7. *What are the economic benefits of using your product?*
If you can say that your product or service will save the user money, time, or effort, you have a great competitive advantage. And, if you can document this with figures in your copy, you'll have a very persuasive story to tell. Don't be afraid to go into the details. If your market is even the least bit cost conscious, they'll read every word of your copy.

## HOW TO FOCUS YOUR COPY FOR THOSE WHO COUNT

Too much ad copy is totally wasted because the writers never know anything about the people who buy the products. There's no substitute for actually talking with prospects and customers to see what motivates them to buy your products or those of your competitors. But if this can't be done, try to get as much information as you can from your salespeople. At first, you will get a lot of information that will more confuse than help you. But, if you dig deeply enough, the threads will emerge.

Talk to a purchasing person, and you'll get the impression that price is most important. But the plant superintendent wants to know if the product will last for a hundred years. Then the engineer wants to know if he can extract a square root from your floor scraper as it does its work. When you see the problems of each, and decide who is more important, and what steps the decision-making process takes, you will have the slant on the people problem of writing copy.

Over the years that I have been writing copy for industrial ads I have found that the most helpful way to view prospects is in terms of three categories: initiators, deciders, and permitters. I'm sure that others have similar names for the same functions, but it all boils down to trying to find out where the power lies.

The *initiator* is the person who starts the ball rolling. It may be the person who circles the bingo number under your ad, or it could be the person who phones in response to your direct mail piece. However, when the initiator plays this role and no other, he is not responsible for saying yes when you ask for the order.

The *decider* is the one who says yes. He or she may be the person who compares the specs on yours and the equipment of others, and then gives the nod. The full responsibility may lie with the decider if he or she also has the power of the permitter.

The *permitter* may never see or use the product, but he or she may be able to block the sale for any number of reasons. For example, consider the situation in which a chemical engineer has initiated interest in an advertised product and gotten tentative approval from his boss, but then finds the controller putting on the squeeze because of a financial condition unknown to the others.

Of course, it's possible for these roles to be played by three individuals, one person, committees, informal groups, and just about any other social structure you can imagine in business. But it's not necessary to know each in detail. All you really need to know is who you want to influence and what will do the job.

Be sure that you know whom you want to influence. Every situation is different, and you can make the most of your advertising dollars if you write to the audience that can be most influential in the sale. Of course, your advertising may require different ads aimed at each member of the decision-making team. It's not uncommon in the chemical industry, for example, to see ads directed to the chemical engineers who appreciate the technical benefits of a particular chemical and initiate the action. Other ads for the same product try to make the purchasing person decide that the chemical is not only the most economical, but that it can be delivered quickly. Yet another ad might be aimed at top management in the firm to convince them that their permission to buy the chemical will have important benefits on the bottom line. Each ad would appear in the publications that would be appropriate for the specific audience.

When you know everything about the product that can affect the sale, you can begin to think about the copy itself. But, before you put any words on paper, there are a few points you should think about. People who have never written advertising tend to think more in terms of gimmicks and tricks than they do of the importance of creating a sales message. Don't think that you have to trick your prospects into reading your ad. Those who read business-publication advertising react negatively when they are bushwhacked by a gimmick. If you give the readers what they want—and they do want information—you are on your way to a sale.

## HOW TO USE THE TEN-STEP COPY PLAN

When you know everything there is to know about the product and the people who will use it, it's time to think about the copy. Most professional copywriters have long since forgotten the details of the checklist that follows; however, they follow it intuitively. If you haven't written copy before, I suggest that you take the easy and safe way: use the list each time you are faced with a piece of copy until it becomes second nature.

This is not a pick-and-choose list. If you skip any point, I guarantee that your copy will be weak. Even if you're not going to write a word yourself, be sure that you know and understand what follows. You're going to have to evaluate someone else's copy, and when you can use the points in this list you will know whether or not you're getting your money's worth.

## The Ten-Step Copy Plan

1. *State the objectives of the ad.*
   Your first job is to determine just what you want to accomplish. Here are the objectives most often associated with advertising copy:

   a. To introduce a new product or a new feature of an existing product.
   b. To explain unique characteristics of the product.
   c. To explain product performance.
   d. To show how the product is used for best results.
   e. To initiate an immediate reader response.
   f. To aid dealers in their sales efforts.
   g. To enhance the brand or corporate image.
   h. To tell of corporate developments that may enhance sales.
   i. To tell of price changes, guarantees, discounts, etc.
   j. To retain a good image when there are problems, such as shortages.

   Choose *one!* Any attempt to feature two or more copy objectives will weaken your ad. You can, of course, make other points in your copy, but every piece of copy you write should have one major objective, and there should be no doubt in the reader's mind what you are trying to say.

2. *Describe the audience for your copy.*
   When you know your readers and what they will respond to, you can write the kind of copy that will

attract their attention. This isn't to say that you would talk down to shipping clerks, and use nothing but scientific lingo if your prospects are biochemists. It simply means that each responds more favorably when you use language that is most familiar.

You can get a good clue to the right slant by reading the magazines in which you plan to run your ads. Read the ads as well as the articles, and soon you will see just what style is appropriate for your copy.

3. *Know when the product is purchased.*
Even though there are few truly seasonal industrial products, there are often times when it's better to advertise than others. For example, if you are selling components to automotive manufacturers, you must reach your prospects during the design phase.

4. *Know how the product is bought.*
If your product is usually bought in certain units, and there are advantages to your way of offering the products, the facts should be included in your copy. And your readers will want to know how you plan to sell to them. Company salespeople? Reps? Distributors? The fact that local stock is available has often made the difference when a competitor must ship from a thousand miles away.

5. *Know why the product is bought.*
Few industrial products are bought to enhance status, but some seemingly insignificant points can make the difference. For example, industrial advertisers usually pay little attention to packaging. But when a product is bought that must be stored by the customer for a while, a package advantage could make the difference.

Don't limit your search for why a product is bought to the usual points—price, quality, etc. Look for other reasons. Despite the lack of interest most manufacturers have in esthetics, it has been shown time and again that when two pieces of ordinary hardware compete head-on, the better-looking product usually wins out. You probably won't want to make this point in your copy, but it sure helps to illustrate a product that makes your competitors look scuzzy. ·

6. *Decide exactly what you want the reader to do.*
Because so few industrial products can be sold directly from a magazine ad, or even a direct mail piece, the objective of most of the copy you write will be to identify prospects. Most often, this is done by getting the readers interested enough so that they will tell you who they are. If you want them to send for a catalog, say so. Tell them to call, write, or circle the bingo number if the magazine has an inquiry processing system. But, and this is important, decide before you write anything that this is where you want to take the reader after he or she has finished reading your copy. If you write with this in mind, your request won't look as though it was tacked on as an afterthought.

7. *List every feature and every benefit.*
Start with the features. List them in a single column, and then list the benefits in a second column. There may be more than one benefit for each feature. Don't give up until you are absolutely sure that you have every benefit, and that you know which benefits will be most important to most of the people who will read your copy. Not all the benefits will be used in your copy, but you should list them before you start writing.

8. *Decide the order in which you will present your benefits.*
Actually, once you have made your major point, the order in which you present your benefits will make very little difference. However, there is a little trick you can use to make sure that your obsessive readers don't try to rank order the points when you don't want them to. Never use numbers when you list benefits. If you want to present the benefits in stacatto fashion, don't number them, but place dots or other typographical elements next to each just to separate them.

9. *Decide on the theme of the ad.*

Ha! You thought that the product was the theme. Sorry, but the theme is a little more than that. When you plan a theme, you relate your major copy benefit to the needs of the prospects. In a sense, the theme pulls together all the points of the copy into one single, favorable impression to accomplish the objective stated in point 1.

10. *Decide on the copy style.*

Straight exposition is the most popular style, not because it is necessarily most effective, but because it's usually the easiest to handle. You might want to try your hand at a case history if you've got the material. Testimonials work well if the person has the credentials and says something that can be directly related to a benefit for your reader. The danger in using a testimonial is to end up with brag-and-boast copy, which is always weak. Some advertisers use cartoons, but this approach is best left to professionals. You can use humor, but it, too, takes a pro to carry it off.

Many advertisers have found that an ad prepared to look like a newsletter is an effective way to get people to read a lot of copy. The newsletter copy should be "newsy," but don't forget that you are writing to sell. If you can get your readers involved in more than just reading, you will have done your copy job well. Try a little quiz and ask your readers to submit answers for prizes. You'll be surprised at how many people will respond. However, there is always the question of whether these people are puzzle hounds or prospects.

## HEADLINES THAT ATTRACT ATTENTION AND BUILD COPY READERSHIP

A copywriter will tell you that it's the job of the headline to attract attention to the ad. An art director will make the same claim for the layout and illustration. Who's right? They're both right, and the most successful ads use both elements to stop the reader and get him or her into the copy. But, for now, let's look at the tricks of the copywriter's art and see how to create winning headlines every time.

Most novices try to be all things to all people when they write headlines. Rope 'em all in with a headline that covers all bases is their philosophy. It just doesn't work. Such headlines must be general, and generalities will attract few readers. The best headlines single out the readers you want to reach. Remember, not every reader of every magazine you choose to advertise in will be a prospect for your products. Therefore, you're always better off striving to reach only those who represent the best prospects.

## How to Attract the Readers Who Count

It's no great trick to get people to respond to an offer of a free catalog. But it's another thing to get a good response from people who are real prospects and who are genuinely interested in your product. To insure that you get more of the latter, you should give a lot of thought to your advertising headlines. If you refer to a need or a problem that your prospects have, you will have narrowed down the range of respondents to those who should have more than a passing interest. And, of course, when a benefit is apparent, you will hear from the best prospects.

A headline will encourage prospects to read the copy when it promises that the product will fill the need or solve a problem. Often the promise is in a subhead; trying to get everything into a single headline can result in too many words. Here are a few examples.

Headline based on a problem:
**Reduce flow measurement error with the model FL-G flow meter**
Subheadline to get reader into copy:
**New sensitive flow meter measures flow as low as .006 GPM**

Headline based on a benefit:

**This needle valve is still leak-tight when the pressure reaches 6,000 psi**

Subheadline to get reader into copy:

**New double O-ring system prevents stem leakage on Ace valves**

Your headlines must be believable. No matter how outstanding your product is, or how far you have extended the operating specifications, if you are vague, you are in trouble. Contrast the following headlines and decide for yourself which is vague and which is believable.

**Reduce your water consumption costs**
**Reduce your water consumption costs by 60%**

**This laboratory shaker gives long-lasting service**
**This laboratory shaker has operated day-in and day-out, 24 hours a day for the last 22 years**

This may seem obvious, but a headline must be understandable. Surprisingly, many headlines really aren't understandable at first glance. Readers may be able to get the idea after they have thought about the words for a while, but by that time they will have turned the page to someone else's ad. Remember, the job of the headline is to attract attention and to compel the reader to go on to the copy. If the reader must question what is meant, the impact is lost. Consider this headline:

**Ace valves get the job done**

This doesn't say much, and it's language that doesn't apply to the use of valves. The writer was trying to say that his valves handle the job of controlling a corrosive fluid that others couldn't. Doesn't this headline make more sense:

**Ace valves handle corrosives—a job that others can't**

Among the myths that abound in the advertising business is the feeling that headlines must always be short in order to be successful. This is just not true. If you have a lot to say, and you say it compellingly, the headline will work. On the other hand, if your goal is to pack everything you have to say in as few words as possible, you will surely weaken your sales message. When ad writers strive for brevity, they are really trying not to be windy. People will read long headlines and long copy as long as you have something to say and write to hold their attention. So, don't try to cut every headline down to three words; instead, strive to make every word count, no matter how long the headline is. How about this short headline:

**Marvel paint gives long-lasting protection**

It's short, but what has been said? "Long-lasting" doesn't really say anything. Wouldn't the same idea be much stronger said this way:

**Marvel paint withstands the rigors of any climate, and is guaranteed not to peel in any weather for two years.**

The second headline has more than three times the words of the first, but it says something. Brevity in copy is important, but don't strip the nerve from your prose just to keep the word count down.

## How to Use the Seven Types of Headlines

Most business advertising headlines fall into these seven categories. Here are a few hints to help you use each most effectively.

1. *The how-to headline*

    People who read business, trade, and professional magazines are looking for answers. When your ad headline promises to tell them how to solve a problem they are having, you will have captured a reader. However, be sure that your copy fulfills the promise, even if the final answer doesn't lie in your copy but in a catalog you will send if the reader requests it, you have fulfilled the promise in the headline. Compare the promise in these headlines:

**Arc resistors can be used in many applications**
**How to choose the right Arc resistor for any application**

The first is a rather bland statement that wouldn't move too many people into the copy. However, if you are an electrical engineer, the second headline promises to tell you how to solve a common engineering problem with Arc resistors.

2. *The news headline*

New and now are words that are so overworked that most readers discount them almost immediately. However, all readers are seeking something new and they want what they want now. It's the clever headline writer who can convey that something new is really new. Consider these two examples:

**New data disc stores 2,000,000 bytes and is indestructible**
**The first data disc to store 2,000,000 bytes—and it's indestructible**

Your product may be new, but anything you can do to get rid of the overworked word "new" will help make your news headlines draw more readers.

3. *The picture-integrating headline*

A strong visual can often be used to tell the story, and all the headline is expected to do is provide the transition to the copy. The headline may just state what is seen in the picture—in terms of benefits, of course—or it can be used to begin the copy.

Suppose you had a photograph of a fork-lift that could lift six pallets side by side. Well planned, the picture tells the story, but you could use a headline such as this:

**Lift six pallets at a time, and think of the time and money you'll save**

This headline restates the obvious, but phrases the message in terms of the time- and money-saving benefits. Don't worry about redundancy in advertising. Every copywriter learns this axiom very early: Tell em' what you're going to tell 'em, tell 'em, and tell 'em what you told 'em.

4. *The prediction headline*

When you use this approach, you will find it most effective to use the second person. That is, use "you." This headline makes a positive prediction and includes a very strong benefit.

**You will recover 64% of your solvent when you install a Smith solvent-recovery plant**

5. *The command headline*

When you can use a commanding statement that is in the reader's best interest, you will have a strong headline. In a sense, the command headline is the prediction headline without the "you." To be most effective, command headlines should be relatively short. Consider this example:

**Cut process time in half with a Stellar heater**

Contrast this with the same concept used as a prediction headline:

**You can cut process time in half with a Stellar heater**

Either approach will work, but your copy should follow the style of the headline. If you use the prediction approach, continue to talk in terms of what will happen when the product is used. The command approach lends itself more to direct copy and a closing that suggests immediate further investigation by the reader.

6. *The testimonial headline*

Most people like to know how others have fared with the product being advertised, and a testimonial can be a productive way of answering the question and getting the copy read. However, be careful that you quote someone who will be respected by the readers. The person may not be well known, but as long as he or she has a position that will be respected, you will be on safe ground. And make sure that the quote sounds natural. If the person being quoted says something inappropriate or out of character (the quote was obviously created by the copywriter), you will have a very weak ad.

Of course, the testimonial doesn't necessarily have to be the words of an individual. If you get permission from a user to say that the company increased production by 60 percent when your product was used, you will have a strong testimonial.

7. *The short story headline*

The short story headline must lead into a short story—or a brief piece of copy that gets the message across in story form. Although the story approach often features people, it is not necessarily used to give testimonials. More often than not, this approach is best used with a human interest angle. For example, a manufacturer of valves could use this headline to lead into a story of how one small component is the key to success for a complex system:

**How one Apex valve keeps this entire processing plant functioning**

This approach works well when the story is told in dialog, whether the copy is based on fact or fiction.

However, if you use this approach to write a head, be sure that the copy follows the same style.

## HOW TO WRITE COMPELLING COPY

Your copy is your sales pitch. The headline and the illustration have gotten the reader interested, and now you must do the selling in the copy. All good copy has four characteristics in common. Let's look at each in some detail.

1. Use the first paragraph, or first few sentences if the copy is only one paragraph long, to build on the interest created in the headline. The first few words are critical, so keep your copy short, to the point, and limited to the major benefit. You've got to reward the reader for moving from your headline to your copy.

2. Every word of your copy must be chosen to arouse a desire for the product or service. If you follow these steps, you will be writing to accommodate the thought processes your reader has when he or she is interested in your product. First, describe the most important features of the product. Be sure that you define this importance in terms of the user's interests, not yours. Next, translate these features into benefits and then show the reader how these benefits will be important to him or her.

3. Be convincing. To do this, be specific, direct, and to the point. Prove our claims with facts. Even though you may be perfectly justified in bragging, don't. Let the facts speak for themselves and your readers will come away with the feeling that you are great but humble.

4. Tell the reader what he or she is expected to do. If your copy was thought out with a goal in mind, you already know what you expect the reader to do when he or she finishes reading the ad. Your ad may be purely institutional, but you still want the reader to go on to the next page with a good feeling about your product. The best way to do this is to reiterate the benefit in terms the

reader understands and let him know that he did the right thing by reading the ad. If you want the reader to call you, say so. You might include an inducement such as a premium for those who call. The best premium for an industrial product is something that will help the reader with his work—something that is related to the product you sell. If, for example, you manufacture valves, you might develop a slide rule or a nomograph that can be used to compute pressure drops across orifices.

If you want the reader to send a coupon, make the coupon obvious and tell the reader to return it—**NOW.** If you want the reader to circle a reader service number under the ad provided by the magazine publisher, don't leave anything to chance. Close the copy with a direct suggestion: "Circle the number below this ad and we will send you our new and complete catalog."

## How Long Can Your Copy Be?

Most people who tell you that people won't read long copy are responding defensively because they never read anything longer than the listings in *TV Guide.* Don't listen to them. Every publisher and every independent readership service says that long as well as short copy is read and acted on. It's not the length that makes the difference, it's what's in it for the reader and how interesting it is. Ten words in the hands of a hack can be tedious, but 1,000 words in the hands of a pro can be a joy to read. However, there is one caution you should observe. If your copy is going to be long, make sure that there is enough space to use a legible typeface. If you're good, but long, copy is going to be set solid in seven-point type, it just won't do the job. As a rule of thumb, try not to use text type any smaller than nine points. Ten- or eleven-point text with one or two points leading (space) between lines works nicely for most ads from a quarter to a full page. See the discussion of typography in Chapter 3.

## How to Write Convincingly

Entire books have been written on this subject, but I'm going to try to give you the essence in a few paragraphs. However, to make it most effective, I'd like to suggest that you read the ads in any one trade magazine from cover to cover after you have read the next few paragraphs. As you read, look for the points I am about to make. See how skillful copywriters have made use of success-tested techniques, and how others have written with little or no understanding of persuasive writing.

1. Write the way your audiences expects you to write. If your audience is accustomed to prepositions at the end of a sentence, forget the rules and use them. And be sure to use the vernacular of the industry. Plumbers call them faucets, and process engineers talk of valves. If you were to write about a faucet in a process control line in a hydrocarbon plant, your readers would laugh.

2. Develop your copy so that you make your main points early and follow up with other facts and substantiating claims in the rest of the copy. If your story must be told in a logical sequence, be sure that no point is out of order. And be sure to build your copy so your closing is anticipated and tells the reader what he has to do to either get the product or more information.

3. Be brief. Write long copy if you like, but keep the sentences to a manageable length. If you have a long compound sentence that can be broken up into two shorter sentences, do it. Some readers will lose the point at the end of a long sentence. Remember, this is a visual world; TV and other visual aids have turned people from readers to viewers.

4. Always use the simplest word. It's not a mark of erudition to use larger words, it just makes reading that much more difficult. Why say compensation, when pay means the

same thing? Expectation conjures up the title of a Victorian novel, when the word hope means the same thing without the confusing connotation.

5. Prune out extraneous words. In a sense, this is part of being brief. But, what I mean here is to slice out the little phrases that can be replaced by single words. For example, if you have written, "In the event that you need extra parts, they will always be available," why not change it to "Extra parts will always be available"? No one is going to buy extra parts unless he needs them, so why waste the words.

6. Use few modifiers and many action words. Adjectives do little for copy, but verbs put your thoughts in motion. Look at some copy that you feel is well written, and I'll bet that you will see very few adjectives but quite a strong dependence on verbs. Compare this headline with the one that follows:

**Scrape, smooth, and finish your walls with one tool**
**Do every wall finishing job with one tool**

Scrape, smooth, and finish are strong verbs that give motion to the line, and they tell specifically what the tool will do. In the second line, the reader is given one verb, and a weak one at that.

7. Use the active voice. When the subject of the verb performs the action, you will have stronger copy than when you use the passive voice in which the subject is acted upon.

When you write, "Engineers say that Smith transducers reduce error by 75%," you are using the active voice, present tense—a strong grammatical construction for copywriting. Compare this with, "It will be found that Smith transducers reduce error by 75%." This is passive voice, future tense. Without getting bogged down in the details of grammar, which sentence do you think would be most effective? The first, of course. Be sure your writing has this flavor, and it will sell. You probably won't have to review English I to write good copy.

8. Don't use abstractions. If you were thinking about buying a laboratory instrument, would you rather read about its versatility, or that the instrument took pH readings, and did a turbidity analysis all at the same time? Abstractions don't leave the reader with strong and realistic images. Even the best copywriters will find them in their first drafts. However, they shouldn't show up after editing.

## LET'S PUT IT ALL TOGETHER

I've given you a lot of rules, hints, and guidelines for writing copy. But the best way to put everything into perspective is to write an ad yourself. If you follow this exercise the first few times you write your copy, it should become second nature, and your copy will have the selling punch it needs to be competitive. Let's write an ad. The product to be advertised is a control valve for the Ace Company.

### The Seven Key Questions to Ask about the Product

1. What is the product made of? Teflon, or 18–8 stainless steel.

2. Construction details? Precision-machined from a forging. Unique straight-through design doubles the life of the valve, compared with competitors' products.

3. What does the product do best? Controls corrosive fluids.

4. How important are competitive differences? Competitors' valves meet the same operating specifications, but this valve lasts twice as long because of straight-through design. It can be shipped from local stock; competitive valves take six weeks for delivery.

5. Where and how can the product be purchased? From a nationwide network of stocking distributors.

6. Do you have a price advantage? No. Valves are priced in the same range as most competitors'.

7. What are the economic benefits of using the product? The valve, because of its design, will outlast all others on corrosive service. The economic benefit is reduced maintenance and replacement cost.

## What is the Copy Focus?

Research has shown that the design engineer in this case is both the initiator and the decider. A final vote must come from the purchasing agent—the permitter. However, the purchasing agent leaves the gathering of competitive prices to the engineer who acts as the initiator and decider. The design engineer is the target.

## Using the Ten-Step Copy Plan

1. State the objective of the ad. The objective of the ad is to explain a unique characteristic—a design feature that doubles the life of the valve, compared with competitive valves.

2. Describe the audience for your copy. Design engineers working on processing plants.

3. When is the product purchased? Specification takes place long before purchasing. However, no one time of the year is important.

4. How is the product bought? By the contractor, but the contractor buys the product specified by the engineering firm doing the design.

5. Why is the product bought? In this case, price is not a problem. Dependable,, and low-maintenance service is the deciding factor.

6. What do you want the reader to do? The advertiser wants the reader to request technical literature, and to identify himself and herself so there can be a sales follow-up.

7. List every feature and benefit that will be used in the ad.

| Features | Benefits |
|---|---|
| 18–8 stainless steel and Teflon construction | Can be used on corrosive fluids Environmental safety |
| Straight-through drilling eliminates wire-drawing, which contributes to corrosive and flow wear | Longer in-service life Lower maintenance and replacements costs |
| Available from local stock | No waiting for delivery |
| Ace meets all government and industrial environmental standards | No need to use expensive added safety equipment |

8. Decide on the order in which the benefits will be presented.
   a. Reduced corrosive wear.
   b. Low maintenance and replacements costs.
   c. No waiting for delivery.
   d. Proven design.
9. Decide on ad theme. The theme will relate the design feature to the problems engineers have with valves that are not designed and built the same way.
10. What is the copy style? A straight narrative form will be used.

## The Headline

Now, let's write the headline. Bear in mind that the headline and the copy could be written in many different ways, and each would probably be as effective as the other, as long as each of the points we have discussed is used. Here's the way I would write it:

Headline:
**How to choose the right valve for corrosive service**
Subheadline:
**Select Ace valves to reduce maintenance costs by 72%**

I've used a how-to format for the headline; it will peak the curiosity of those the valve manufacturer wants to reach. The subheadline identifies the product and promises a strong, direct benefit: save 72 percent on maintenance costs.

The copy must be written to follow the image created by the headline and the subhead. Here's how I would handle it:

> Corrosive fluids pass straight through Ace valves, not through flow-reducing and wear-producing angular passages found in most other valves. Because of this unique design, wear is reduced by 50% and you will save as much as 72% on maintenance costs. Today, when problems of contamination are especially important, you must specify valves that not only control flow, but protect the environment as well. The patented Ace design, coupled with parts precision-made of 18–8 stainless steel and Teflon, meet all industry and government environmental standards. We have 12 warehouses all over the country that will deliver any number of the over 200 valves listed in our catalog. Circle the reader service number below and we'll send you a catalog. Or, if you're in a hurry, call us on this toll-free number. We can send you a catalog just as quickly as we can send you a valve.

Now, ask these questions about the copy: Is there a strong promise, and is the copy believable? Is it understandable? What about length? This copy is about as long as it should be for a full-page ad in a 7 x 10 inch magazine. Did I make use of appropriate vernacular and were complex words eliminated in favor of simpler words? Are there any unsupported generalities? And what about the use of active verbs?

Try it yourself. Go back to the facts I made up to fill out the copy plan and the answers to the seven product questions and write your own headline, subheadline, and copy. It could be entirely different from mine, but if you follow all of the suggestions I have made in this chapter, it will probably be just as effective.

## HOW TO FIND AND WORK WITH FREE-LANCE COPYWRITERS

You can have an in-house agency and buy some or all of your copy outside. As I mentioned in previous chapters, everyone starts a house agency for different reasons. If your reason is economic and you feel your interests are best served by buying creative work outside, don't hesitate to buy the best. Actually, the best is seldom that much more expensive than average copy. But you will see a big difference in the results.

I think it's best to tell you first where you shouldn't look for copywriting. As you can see, copywriting is a very structured and disciplined form of writing. Those who write successful novels would probably fail at writing copy, just as the copywriter would find it difficult to turn out a bestseller.

Perhaps English teachers are the worst people to talk with for your copy needs. For the most part, they are usually quite bright, know their grammar, and can discuss Chaucer for hours on end. But their background seldom includes experience in writing persuasive copy. And people whose experience is mainly academic are usually more concerned with grammar than with the practical matter of using words to sell. Of course, I'm sure that many English teachers have become fine copywriters, but if you choose such a person, make sure that his or her copywriting experience is recent and strong.

It isn't necessary for the copywriter you choose to have experience with exactly the same product that you make. But your writer should understand your technology, your product, and your market. A good industrial or technical copywriter is usually able to make the switch from chemistry to electronics quickly and still turn out strong selling copy. But I think you'll find it difficult dealing with a writer who has done little more than handle copy for a department store if your copy needs are technical.

You may want to work with an individual writer, or you may find it convenient to use the creative department of a full-service advertising agency. Most agencies that provide clients with a total service will also handle clients on a project basis. That is, they offer what is known as boutique services. You simply buy the services you need.

If your house agency was formed mainly to control the media placement for the 15 percent commissions, you will probably find it advantageous to work with an agency for all of your creative services. Doing this, you will have the convenience of having all of the creative work handled by one group. You won't have to deal with individual writers and artists. Of course, everyone's needs and goals are different, but most house agencies that farm out all their creative work prefer this arrangement.

Even if you are buying only copy services, it may still be economical and productive to buy it on a project basis from a full-service agency. The agency can usually offer the service of several writers. This can be a benefit when you need copy in a hurry or prefer a fresh point of view.

Many free-lancers offer copywriting services exclusively, and many of them are very good. Those who have lasted are generally excellent writers who prefer the freedom of being on their own as well as the opportunity to control their income and time.

The free-lancers I know and have worked with have all had several characteristics in common. I think you should know a little something about them before you buy free-lance copy:

1. Most free-lancers are not "team" players. At first you may find them self-centered and feel that they appear inflexible, but this is seldom the case. Working in any company environment, whether it's an ad agency or any other kind of business, requires making some concessions. When a strong-willed client insists that the copy be written his way, it takes a strong writer to turn the situation around. However, the impetus to knuckle under usually comes from agency people who can see the 15 percent vanishing if the client's words aren't run as is. The free-lancers who have survived and become successful are less likely to do this. They know their own worth, and they know that

there are enough people who want good copy so that they don't have to be foils. The best advice I can give you is to respect them and don't be a second-guesser. When the writer knows that you have faith in him or her and respect the work being done, you will get the best effort. Think of a free-lance copywriter as you would any other professional, such as your lawyer or doctor. Take your writer's advice. If you have no faith, don't try to rewrite every word, get a new writer. After all, you'd do the same with a doctor.

2. The best copywriters are quite versatile. In the consumer marketing business, copywriters get pegged as beer or cigarette writers and seldom get any other kind of assignments. Writing consumer copy is much more lucrative than writing industrial and business copy, so most of them cherish this reputation and trade on it to keep their prices up. However, most industrial, technical, and business copywriters can switch from one product to another relatively easily. Don't be dismayed if you have to explain your product in detail to your free lancer the first time. However, by the second meeting if the writer still asks the same basic questions, you should think about looking for another.

3. There are no benchmarks that you can use to judge all copywriters. Some were engineers, others did teach English. Others never went to college, and some find it difficult to spell the same word the same way twice. The best way to judge them is by their copy and the successes they have had. If you read their samples, keeping in mind the copywriting points I have made in this chapter, you should be able to make a good choice. One first-rate writer I know never went to college and used to operate a gift store. Another holds a Ph.D. and formerly taught history.

4. Each is very much an individual. Don't expect to deal with them the way you might deal with a writer employed full-time by an ad agency. However, this kind of

individualism is what makes life interesting for them and for those for whom they work. Judge them by their work, not by the fact that they show up at your office in jeans, not a business suit.

## What Should You Pay for Copy?

How high is up? There are no fixed standards, and the way our economy has been inflating for the past few years makes it even more difficult to give you workable guidelines. However, you will find it better to ask for a fixed estimate for every job rather than to ask the writer for his or her hourly rate.

In 1979, I figured my hourly rate at $65. To some, this may sound high; to others quite low. But if you figure that I could research and write a full-page ad in about 3 hours, the charge of $195 doesn't seem high. However, if I had quoted the $65 per hour rate without a time figure, most smaller clients would have gone elsewhere.

You are much better off not even asking about the hourly rate; just get a firm quote for the job.

## How to Find Good Copywriters

A lot of full-time copywriters moonlight on their off-time. You can find them by asking magazine advertising sales representatives for leads, or by getting in touch with a local advertising club, if one exists. Many of the moonlighters do their work with the blessings of their employers and others do it against their wishes. Be sure that you know which situation exists. If your writer handles competitive products during the day at the agency that employs him, but is willing to work for you, you would be well advised to avoid the situation. Sooner or later you and the writer will be in for trouble.

Local universities that offer advertising courses are often able to supply the names of their instructors, many of whom have worked or are still working in the field.

If you're not near an area where copywriters may live, you can still get good service, but it will come via the post office.

Many excellent writers supply copy by mail. These writers have developed their approach so that they can get all the information they need either over the phone, or with a simple printed form. Don't be afraid to deal with a writer through the mail. Some of the best of them have purposely removed themselves from the gut-busting cities where the advertising business thrives to be where they want to be and do their work in peace.

Here are some sources you can use to locate free-lance copywriters:

**Business and Professional Advertising Association**
205 East 42nd Street
New York, NY 10017
(212) 661–0222

This 3,000-member organization is made up of communications professionals who work in industrial, trade, business, and professional marketing. There are a number of local chapters, and you should be able to get a few names from the local chapter secretaries.

**Advertising Age**
740 North Rush Street
Chicago, IL 60611
(312) 649–5200

*Advertising Age*, a weekly magazine, carries classified advertising of free-lancers and moonlighters in each issue. It's more consumer than industrial marketing oriented, but they do carry major articles of interest to industrial marketers.

**Industrial Marketing**
740 North Rush Street
Chicago, IL 60611
(312) 649–5260

This magazine is published for those who sell products and services to business and industry. You will find small ads occasionally run by free-lancers.

**Direct Marketing**
224 Seventh Street
Garden City, NY 11530
(516) 746–6700

This is your best source for direct mail copywriters. The magazine has a regular section in the back that lists many free-lance direct mail writers.

In larger cities where many advertising agencies exist, you will probably find a number of writers listed in the yellow pages. Talk with as many as you can, and be sure to ask for samples of their work as well as the names of individuals and companies for whom they have worked.

# Chapter 6

# How to Design Your Own Ads, or Buy from Free-Lancers and Save

If there's one place where the average in-house agency falls down, it's in layout and art. With some effort, most people can learn to apply the principles of copywriting, and it's not especially difficult to learn how to plan and buy printing. But, if you don't have a sense of visual organization, your ads will look like those found in every high school yearbook.

It's not necessary to be able to do finished renderings or drawings, or even to be able to take good photographs. But it is important to understand the visual principles that attract and hold readers' attention. Surprisingly, many excellent art directors can't draw. If they had to prepare a rendering they would be lost. But they understand the principles of composition as they relate to advertising and can apply them with an unfailing eye.

So, if you failed the matchbook art test and were rejected by a mail-order art school, don't give up—yet. However, if after reading this chapter you still feel uneasy, I suggest that you find a good free-lancer, boutique, studio, or even an agency willing to undertake individual assignments and have your art and layouts done professionally. You'll be in good company; many successful in-house agencies have gone this route.

## HOW TO PREPARE A LAYOUT

Ads are created by combining copy and illustrations in a way that not only attracts attention, but pulls the reader's eye through each element to a logical conclusion. There are times when an illustration is used to attract attention and others when it's the headline. No one can say categorically that a headline or an illustration is always the most important element, except those writers or artists with tunnel vision who are personally threatened when their work doesn't dominate. The layout lets you work out how much weight to give the various elements in your ad.

An advertising layout is much like the blueprint your engineering department prepares when it plans to manufacture a product. The layout tells where the elements of the ad will appear, how they relate to each other in order to create interest and hold attention, and what form of illustration will be used. Illustrations are sketched in roughly, copy is indicated with ruled lines, and the headline is usually lettered in rough form.

Let's follow an idea through the various layout stages to see just what happens at each step. The product is paint. The art director was given a headline and copy, and told to create several layout possibilities. In all cases, the can of paint was to dominate because the logo on the label was prominent and the advertiser thought that brand identification was important.

The headline is:

**These walls were painted for 3¢ a square foot**

The subhead is:

**... 50% lower than anyone expected.**

The layout artist first did a few *thumbnail sketches.* These are mini-layouts, done in the same proportion as the finished ad is to be, but with loose sketching and no attempt at detail. In many agencies the thumbnails are shown only in the art department because it is felt that non-art people have difficulty visualizing the᾿ idea. There is a lot of justification for this. Architects often do the same thing, refusing to show their clients their thumbnail sketches.

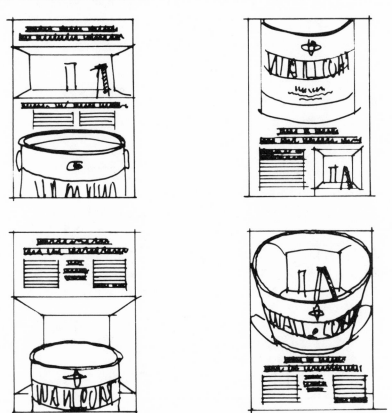

Figure 6-1   Thumbnail layouts

After the layout artist, or others in the art department, selects a thumbnail that appears to offer the best possibilities, a *rough layout* is prepared. The rough will probably include some changes suggested when the thumbnails were reviewed, but roughs are still loose and lacking in detail. However, these layouts are done in the same size in which the finished ad will appear.

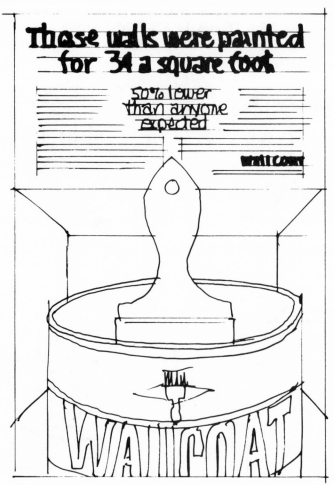

Figure 6-2    Rough layout

The rough layout seldom goes out of the art department, either. It's used by the art director and others in the creative department for a final review before a finished layout is prepared.

The *finished layout* is rendered in considerable detail. The headline is carefully lettered, and the sketch of the illustration should leave little to the imagination. Display type may be set, but the copy is still represented by ruled lines. However, the area occupied by the text copy will be carefully copy-fit so that when the type is set and positioned in the mechanical, it will occupy the exact space that was alloted to it on the layout.

**Figure 6-3    Finished layout**

If those who have the responsibility of approving ads can visualize from a rough layout, this may be as far as the layout process will go. However, most non-artists prefer something with more detail before they give their approval.

If a tighter presentation is required, a *comprehensive layout* will be prepared. This layout is either very tightly rendered, or it can be prepared with photostats of the illustrations positioned in place, along with a paste-up of the headline and copy set in type.

Figure 6-4   Comprehensive layout

Comprehensives are expensive. However, if those who must approve the ad want to see it in detail, it's often the best way to go. If changes must be made on a finished ad that was approved in final layout form and then prepared in finished mechanical form, the costs will be much higher. And there is usually considerable time lost.

## THE PRINCIPLES OF ADVERTISING LAYOUT

As I said in the chapter on copywriting, benefits are what sell products. Readers thumbing the pages of a magazine are looking for information that will help them in some way. They are not especially interested in your new plant, unless you can show them—quickly—how it will be of some benefit. The principles of advertising layout are based on classic art concepts, applied to selling products and services.

Good layouts are simple, contain as few elements as possible, and have an underlying format that moves the reader's eye step-by-step to where it should be taken. If a mathematician had to generate a probability model of the number of combinations of elements that are possible in a single ad, he or she would probably give up. However, a trained artist can immediately reduce the number of possibilities to a few simple approaches because he or she knows what works and what doesn't. If you haven't had any art training and are depending on those who have, take my advice and don't second-guess them. If you don't have confidence in their work, it's best to get someone else and trust that person, rather than to try to impose your ideas on a trained professional.

*Balance* The first thing non-artists think of when balance is discussed is an even distribution of elements on a page That is, if you were to fold a balanced ad in half vertically, the elements on both sides would be equal. This is one form of balance, but it is, by far, the least interesting. However, it's also possible to balance visual elements asymmetrically on a page by varying their size and weight. Weight refers to the relative lightness or darkness that is used.

Look at this seesaw. It illustrates physical balance, but also shows how much more interesting an illustration can be when informal balance is used. One element dominates and the other provides visual support for it. In a formally balanced layout, the reader often has difficulty determining the most important element, unless it is skillfully handled.

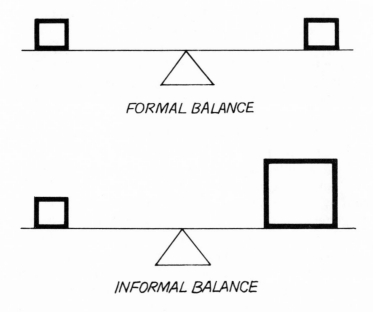

FORMAL BALANCE

INFORMAL BALANCE

Figure 6-5    Visual balance

Balance is considered when relations between left and right sides of the ad as well as top and bottom must be planned. However, the horizontal middle of an ad is not midway between the top and the bottom. The optical center, which is $2/5$ of the way down from the top of an ad, is the point where the reader's eye is usually attracted. Ads that are divided in half between the top and bottom are static and uninteresting. However, when the $2/5 - 3/5$ formula is used, your ads will be much more alive.

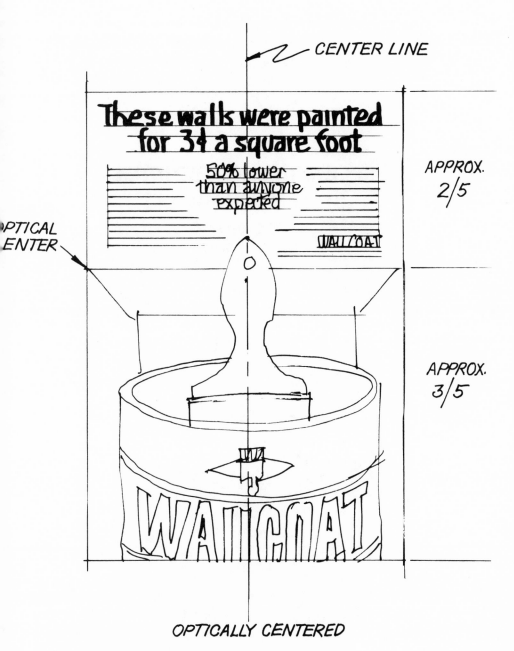

Figure 6-6 The optical center of an ad

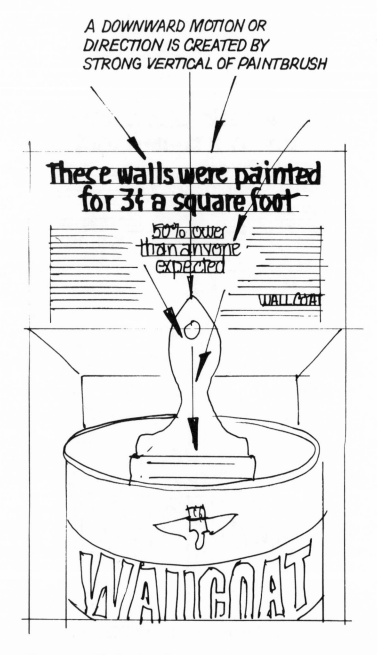

Figure 6-7    Motion in a layout

*Motion* A good layout has motion. The elements are placed so that one element logically pulls the reader to the next in a planned sequence. When a model is used, having the person face the next element forces this motion. The use of shapes that pull the eye from one element to the next is most commonly used in industrial advertising. Psychologists, using sophisticated recording cameras, have been able to determine how this eye flow works, and they have

Figure 6-8 Consistency in a layout

shown that an ad that is poorly designed is confusing, and often causes the reader to leave it before he finishes reading it.

Consistency  Some layouts must have a number of elements, but unless the designer arranges them so they hang together, the ad will resemble a patchwork and the reader will be confused. Joining elements and introducing motion in the layout can prevent this from happening.

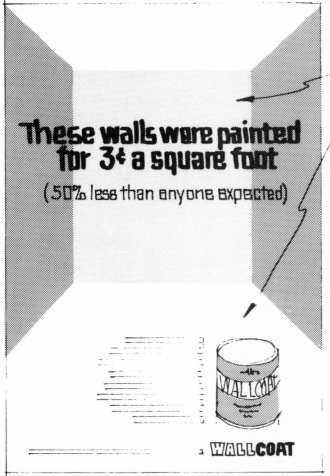

VAST OPEN AREAS SUGGEST LARGE AMOUNTS OF WALL SPACE COVERED FOR SMALL COST AND DRAW ATTENTION TO PRODUCT IN BOTTOM RIGHT HAND CORNER.

These walls were painted for 3¢ a square foot

(50% less than anyone expected)

WALLCOAT

Figure 6-9  The use of white space as a design element

*White space*  Some advertisers feel that white space was meant to be filled. They reason that if they are paying for space, they should put lots of ink on it and every inch should do something to sell. This may work with supermarket ads in newspapers, but for most industrial ads, a judicious use of white space helps gain more attention than a lot of ink. You should think of white space as being as

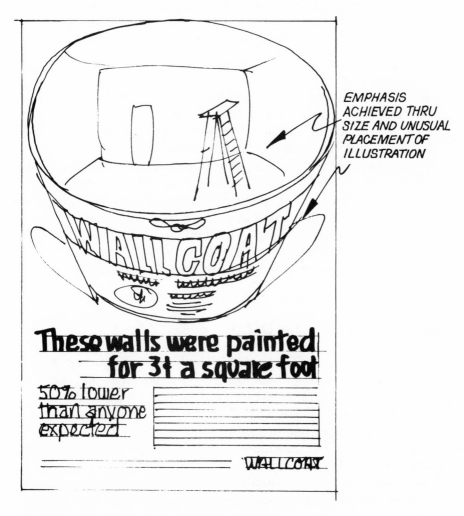

Figure 6-10  The use of emphasis in a layout

much an element of design as the material that is to be printed.

*Emphasis*  When every element of a layout is emphasized, nothing stands out. However, when some elements are arranged to support a main element, whether it's the headline, an illustration, or the copy, the ad will have the strength of emphasis. One of the best ways to emphasize an element is by contrast. Something black against a white background has emphasis, for example. Something small, but strategically placed against white space, will stand out.

*Color*  Today more than ever, industrial advertisers are using color in their ads. Process color is used for emphasis and to illustrate something as it really appears. But one or two colors used in addition to black can often attract as much attention as a more expensive process color ad. Simply because you may have decided to use color, don't splash it around thinking that sheer quantity will do the job. It won't. Think of an ad with a stark white background, a short headline, and only a few lines of copy. However, the product, which is small in relation to the other ad elements, is the only thing shown in color. That use of color will do more to attract attention and leave a good impression than all of the lightning bolts an amateur artist could conjur up.

## HOW LAYOUTS ARE USED

As I mentioned, the layout is the blueprint, the plan for an ad. Once the concept has been approved, it's necessary to convert the sketch into something that can be printed.

First, type will have to be set. Today most type is set by photographic equipment, although many type shops still use Linotype and other mechanical systems. The graphic experts will argue endlessly over small points, but for your purposes, there will be virtually no qualitative differences between type set by these two systems. Many printing plants offer typographic services, but unless you contact a large plant, you will probably

get a broader selection of type from a typographer who specializes in setting type.

Type must be selected to fit the layout, and to complement
the illustration and design. (See the discussion of typography in
Chapter 3). It's best to avoid novelty type for both text and
headlines, and to stick with faces that are familiar and relatively
easy to read. The sans serif faces—those without the embellishments at the ends of the strokes—are probably easiest for the
non-artist to handle. And, it's difficult to go wrong with most
sans serif faces in most industrial ads. You can select them
condensed, expanded, *italic,* **bold,** and light, to suit your layout.

In order to determine whether or not your copy will fit in
the space you have allocated in the layout, you will have to
count all the characters in the typewritten text. Then, after you
have selected a typeface and a size that appears right for the
layout, measure the length of the line your text will occupy.
Next, count the number of characters in a line of type that is the
same length as the length of the line in your layout and divide it
into the total number of characters you have in the manuscript.
This will tell you how many lines of text you will have. This
process is described in detail in Chapter 3.

You may have ended up with a perfect fit, but this may not
be the best way to set the type. Type that is set solid, positioned
with no additional space between the lines, can be difficult to
read. Since you are always fighting for a reader's attention, it's
best to do everything you can to keep him or her reading, and
this usually means adding a small amount of space between each
line. This is called leading, a term derived from the hot metal
days of typesetting. The printer would actually add a strip of
lead between each line to provide the space. However, in
phototypesetting, the process is done electro-optically. But the
term prevails, and leading is measured in points, each point
being the equivalent of $1/72$ of an inch. One, two, or three points of
lead between lines of text copy in sizes up to 12 or 14 points give
a lightness that makes it easier for the reader to get your message.

When you get the type it will be on either photo or
reproduction paper and you will have to paste it down on a
white board that has been ruled (in blue pencil so the lines won't

appear on the negative) to the finished size of the ad. The other elements of the ad are also positioned as indicated on the layout.

Illustrations that have continuous tone, whether they are photographs or drawings, must be reproduced by the halftone process that was described in Chapter 3. You can save a little money by having Velox, or halftone prints, made to the exact size they will appear in the ad and pasting them in position on the mechanical. When this is done, the negative maker will have only one shot to make. It won't be necessary to have the art screened and stripped in an added expense.

Most magazines will accept 120 or 133 line screens, but some tabloid publications printed on news stock require coarser halftone screens. Don't guess what is wanted. Check the print production section of *Standard Rate and Data Service* (a directory of trade publications—see the Appendix for information on the publisher) or contact the publication and ask them to send you a copy of their mechanical requirements.

Line work doesn't require halftone screening. And if it's done in the same size as it's to appear in the ad, it can be pasted right in place to simplify the negative-making process. If it has been done larger, but in proportion, it's a simple matter of having a reproduction photostat made to the right scale and then pasting it in position.

Most magazines print by offset today. This means that they will want negatives of your mechanical, not the cumbersome and expensive-to-ship plates that were required when letterpress was the dominant method of reproduction. However, some publications will ask for positive transparencies, or negatives, and others will want Velox prints or the actual artwork. Be sure that you know what is needed and supply it exactly as specified. If a magazine has to make a conversion from a positive to a negative, for example, they will bill you for the cost of the work.

Be sure to send your negatives to the magazines in well-protected mailers. Corrugated envelopes, reinforced with sheets of chip board, are the best. But mark the envelopes "Photographs, do not bend," just to be sure.

Don't just slip the negative directly into your corrugated envelope; protect both the emulsion and film base sides with a soft paper. Negatives can be scratched easily.

## HOW TO BUY ART FROM PROFESSIONALS

Note that I used the word professionals. Beware of your cousin and your partner's brother-in-law who took an art course once. Also, just as there's as big a difference between a copywriter and a novelist, there is as much of a difference between a commercial artist and one who studied the old masters. Many can cross the lines in both cases, but for your purposes you should seek out people who are making a living in the applied field: commercial art.

Some artists work for and by themselves as free-lancers. Some do it full-time and others moonlight while working during the day for someone else. Your choice should be made first on the basis of the quality of work done and second on the availability of the person you choose. It's occasionally difficult to get hold of moonlighters when you need them, but if you find one who's good, it can pay to put up with the inconvenience.

There are also studios that do work for agencies as well as advertisers. Unless they are large, these studios tend to specialize in certain types of work. For example, you wouldn't choose a studio with strong fashion experience to do your boiler artwork. However, don't look for a group that has done exactly the same kind of work that you have. They may feel it's a conflict, but more important, such direct experience is seldom important. A good artist who specializes in industrial work will find it just as easy to render a transistor as a spark plug.

Ad agencies will also contract to handle the art portion of your work. However, some agencies don't have their own art departments and farm out all their work. If this is the case, you will be paying a middle-person fee for handling. This may be worthwhile if a lot of go-between work is necessary, but it's usually best to work directly with the people who will do the actual work.

Prices are so varied from place to place and person to person, that it's impossible to give you any idea of what you should pay. The best advice I can give is to ask several people you feel might be competent to quote on the same job. But remember, it's not always the best move to choose the lowest bidder. The lowest bidder may be slow and take on your work just to keep things going. And the lowest bidder may be slow because he or she just isn't competent. However, if you insist on seeing work that has been done for others, you should be able to rule out these people.

A word of caution. Don't try to influence your artist's work by showing him or her sketches you may have done, or by parading out a pile of tear sheets of ads done by others that you admire. If you want the full creative input you can get from an artist, just tell him or her what you want the ad to do and paint a word picture of the styles that seem to be effective in the magazines. You might give the artist a few copies of back issues of the magazines in which the ads will run, but to insist on a style is to get less than you are paying for.

Most artists work on an hourly basis, but you should ask them to give you a quote on what it would cost to do the job you have in mind. With this ballpark figure, you can see if your budget will support the work.

That's the short course. It won't make you an artist, but it will give you an idea of what to look for when you buy from a professional. If you do have some talent and training, the suggestions I have offered in this chapter as well as those on printing and production should give you enough background to do some or all of your own ads. However, in the art area as in no other, if you're not with it, get professional help.

# Chapter 7

# How to Plan and Manage a Media Program

The chances are you know the magazines that serve your field and you have already decided which will be best for your advertising. As you envision the process, it's just a matter of getting the rates and sending insertion orders to tie in with relevent special issues. Perhaps a little schmooz with the space salespeople will help get your quarter page up front once in a while and you might even spring for an occasional trade show issue if the publisher agrees to run your new product release.

Easy, isn't it?

Not quite that easy. Believe it or not, though, this is how a lot of media plans come about.

Media selection usually begins with a subjective evaluation, but if you're going to get your money's worth, you need a lot more information. Much of it will come from space salespeople, but if you rely totally on them, you're likely to become confused. It's not that they are unreliable, it's just that there is much more to consider than your personal feelings or pitches from magazine reps. And even before you think of magazines at all, you must develop a media strategy that relates your marketing plans to advertising.

## HOW TO DEVELOP A MEDIA STRATEGY

Before you think about which books (advertising slang for "magazines") will be better than others, you should go back to your marketing plan and determine what your advertising is expected to do. These are the major goals of advertising programs, in order of importance:

1. Increase sales

2. Establish a product image

3. Create market awareness

4. Provide backup for sales staff or distributors

5. Continue a level of awareness

6. Create awareness for a new product or brand

When you decide which of these elements will be most important in your program, you are in shape to think about developing a media strategy. Let's take a look at the major considerations.

1. *Who are the people you most want to reach?*
   It's not enough to say electrical engineers if you are selling test equipment, for example. The EE's who make up your market may be power-generation people and would never read a book that claims strong circulation to people with this general description, but who are working with microwaves. You should know something about the way they buy or specify equipment. Does the prospect have the power to purchase, or is his or her role mainly one of recommendation?

2. *Is timing important for the sale of the product?*
   Some products are seasonal, and others require a long lead time for specification. For example, those selling construction supplies are usually affected by seasonal

conditions. Products for educational markets are bought more heavily at certain times than others. Knowing the buying habits of your prospects will help you make the best media timing decisions.

3. *How often are the ads to be run?*
This ties in with timing, but there are many other factors that should be considered. Some products require steady exposure to keep sales up, and others need only an occasional kick of the wheel to keep things going. New products are usually advertised more frequently than those in the retentive stage. And a strong thrust by a competitor may require a heavier schedule than would ordinarily be considered.

4. *How are the prospects to be reached?*
Should the ads be fractionals and run frequently, or should the same amount of money be allocated to fewer, but larger ads? Will a second color be effective? What about process color? Should special position be bought, or will any location be OK?

After media strategy has been determined, the next step is to evaluate the publications that cover your field. If you don't know all of them, the best place to get the picture is in the business publication edition of *Standard Rate and Data Service.* Published by Standard Rate and Data Service, 5201 Old Orchard Road, Skokie, IL 60077, this monthly directory lists all of the technical, scientific, business, industrial, merchandising, and professional publications in the United States as well as many international magazines. Initially, the best way to begin your search is in the Classification Grouping index. It'll only take a few minutes to scan all the headings to note the areas that will be of interest. Then, turn to each section and read the details of each magazine. I'm going to get into this in some detail later in the chapter, but before I do, there are a few concepts you should understand in order to make intelligent media decisions.

## THE BASICS OF MEDIA EVALUATION

All of the techniques used to evaluate media try to get rid of the apples and oranges problem that can exist in a subjective review. One way of putting each publication on a common footing is to use cost-per-thousand figures. This system tells you how much it costs to reach 1,000 readers, regardless of the total number of readers or the space cost. If, for example, your ad costs $1,000 in one magazine, and the circulation is 100,000, the cost to reach a thousand readers is $100. Even though this reduces one variable to a common concept, you must remember that not every one of the 100,000 readers will see the ad you run in the publication.

It's possible to judge publications after the fact by evaluating the cost to develop an inquiry. When cost-per-inquiry is used, the results should be based on the same ad in different magazines serving the same audience. If the $1,000 ad pulled 250 inquiries in one magazine, the cost per inquiry is $4. However, even this measure must be used with care. I've seen the same ad run in different issues of one publication pull vastly different amounts of inquiries. Normally, however, an ad will pull about the same number of inquiries each time it is rerun in the same publication, if it appears only a few times.

The next concept you should understand is reach. Reach is defined as the number of different individuals who are exposed to at least one of your ads over a period of time. If your media plan can be shown to reach four out of five of the universe you consider to be your market, your plan has a reach of eighty.

Frequency, another media variable, is the number of times your message is delivered within a specific time period.

You will want to know the circulation of the publications you are considering. This is the total number of copies of a single issue of the publication. Controlled-circulation publications are distributed free to individuals who meet the qualifications established by the publisher. Magazines that charge for subscriptions are called paid-circulation books.

The primary audience is defined as the number of readers who buy or receive controlled-circulation copies of the magazine. When those who receive the magazines give them to others, another audience is created—the secondary, or pass-along audience. When a publisher talks of total audience, it is a combination of primary and secondary audiences, or all of the readers of an individual issue.

The primary audience can be documented, and it is done by the various circulation auditing services, but the secondary audience is more difficult to nail down. However, the research techniques used today are sophisticated enough so that you can usually rely on the estimates.

## PSYCHOLOGY AND MEDIA PLANNING

Psychologists have good news and bad news for media planners. The bad news is that after twelve hours people forget about 60 percent of what they have just learned. And most of that forgetting takes place almost immediately after the learning. But the good news is that memory increases with repetition. The message for the media planner is, don't shoot for reach at the expense of frequency. The most successful advertisers have demonstrated that the broader exposure that results from greater frequency is usually worth more than the big image.

Few industrial advertisers have the money to go for reach and frequency. Those who narrow their target and concentrate on frequency are often the most successful. To do this, you may advertise to fewer markets, concentrating your campaign on those known to be most productive. You might even limit your advertising to the products that are most profitable, letting the others ride the coattails of the successful ones. And you might consider using fewer publications, but with greater frequency than you would have considered with more books (magazines) on the schedule.

A recent survey I conducted showed that ad readership in industrial magazines varied quite a bit, depending on the size of the ad. These are the average figures:

| Ad size | Inquiries |
|---------|-----------|
| ¼ | 55 |
| ⅓ | 66 |
| ½ | 92 |
| ⅔ | 99 |
| full | 124 |

Considering that most publications sell a full page for less than four times the cost of a quarter page ad, you might think it best to buy the full and get all those inquiries. But let's look at this from a cost-per-inquiry point of view. Consider these rates taken from the *Standard Rate and Data Service* for a prestigious magazine in the chemical field:

| ¼ page | $585 |
|--------|------|
| full page | $2,340 |

The cost to produce the 55 inquiries with the quarter-page ad is $10.63, while the cost to produce the 124 inquiries with the full-page ad is $18.87.

It costs almost twice as much to produce the inquiries with the full-page ad, and the advertiser has cut the exposure frequency from four to one. Remember what I said about memory and repetition. The quarter-page ads will do more for the budget, the memory, and the sale of the product when you think of frequency instead of reach.

Of course, there are times when big space is called for. You just may want the effect of the big image you get with large space, or you may be introducing a new product or fighting a head-to-head, short-term competitive battle. But, in most advertising situations, think of frequency before you go for reach.

When you narrow down the number of books you use, and increase the frequency with smaller space ads, you may find yourself running more than one ad in each issue in which you advertise. No problem! In fact, it's been shown that advertisers who run more than one ad in the same issue enjoy a higher readership score—by 9.2 percent on average—than do advertisers who run only one full-page ad per issue. On the average, 14 percent of the advertisers in specialized business magazines have more than one ad per issue.

## HOW TO EVALUATE MEDIA

In general, the main goal of media evaluation is to find publications that reach the most people in organizations where the product to be advertised could be used. It's important to define these readers in terms of job function and the amount of influence they have in making purchasing decisions. And, of course, the cost to reach them must be considered.

You should request media kits from all the publications you consider, but you can get most of the basic information that will be helpful in *Standard Rate and Data Service* (SRDS).

The magazines listed in SRDS have completed a standardized questionnaire that gives the basic information a potential advertiser needs. Here's how to use this data:

> *Section 1: Personnel.* This section lists the editors, publishers, and production and advertising people at the publication. If you have advertising questions, contact the advertising director. For print production questions, talk with the production manager. And you can talk with the editor to plan feature articles and discuss your product and corporate publicity.

> *Section 2: Representatives and Branch Offices.* Look here for the name of the advertising representative nearest you.

> *Section 3: Commission and Cash Discount.* The publication's terms are stated here. Most publications grant a 15 percent commission to agencies, including house agencies established as I described in Chapter 2. Most publications used to offer a 2 percent discount for payment in ten days, but this practice is rapidly giving way to net thirty-day terms. And it's not uncommon to see the 15 percent commission granted only when payment is made within thirty days. If you are counting on collecting the agency commission with your house shop, be sure you know which

publications demand thirty-day payment in return for the discount.

*Sections 4, 5, 6, 7: Rates.* These sections describe rates for various size ads and different frequency schedules as well as the charge for color and cover position within the periodical. Read the rate information carefully in Section 5. There are enough variations from publication to publication to cause misunderstandings unless you are very careful. For example, some publications offer discounts for schedules of different frequencies based on only one size ad, while others offer a bulk discount for the total amount of space used, regardless of the sizes of the ads.

*Section 8: Inserts.* At times it pays to run a bulletin or a catalog as part of a publication. When the printed material is supplied to the publisher as an insert, different rates are charged.

*Section 9: Bleed.* Ads that run to the edge of the page are charged at a higher rate. Bleed is seldom practical for anything smaller than a full-page ad, and then it's rarely used unless the ad is in color. According to a recent survey, the use of bleed increases readership by an average of only 3 percent. Some publications don't charge extra for bleed, but many charge between 10 and 15 percent extra.

*Section 10: Special Position.* Unless you specify where you want your ad placed, it will be run wherever it's most convenient for the publisher. For the privilege of selecting a special position, you will pay 10 to 15 percent more, based on the cost of the ad. Some magazines require that special position be bought for a certain number of issues before the order will be accepted. Special position can be an effective way to gain exposure. If, for example, the magazine you use carries a regular column on a topic that relates to your produce or service, and you can arrange to be on the page facing it for the extra charge, it can be money well spent.

*Section 11: Classified and Reading Notices.* The rates for classified advertising, if the magazine carries it, are shown in this section.

*Section 12: Split-run.* Some publishers run several editions of their magazines. The rates and descriptions of the splits will be found in this section.

*Section 13: Special Issues.* Directories, show issues, and other editions on special topics that are not part of the regular publication cycle are included in this section.

*Section 13a: Geographic and/or Demographic Editions.* When different issues are published to reach special groups or geographical areas, the information on them is found in this section.

*Section 14: Contract and Copy Regulations.* The listings in SRDS refer the reader back to a section in the front of the publication that lists 37 points, in small type, that you should read very carefully. These points detail the advertiser's and the publisher's rights and obligations when contracting for the publication of advertising. Read every one of these points before you send an insertion order.

*Section 15: Mechanical Requirements.* This section provides a summary of the printing and production requirements of the magazine. However, for detailed production information, use the companion SRDS *Print Media Production Directory.*

*Section 16: Issue and Closing Dates.* Most magazines close their forms thirty days before the date of issue, but there is enough variation so that you should check before you send an insertion order. You will find the cancellation dates in this section, too. For the most part, you will have to pay for space cancelled after the closing date, even though it isn't used.

*Section 17: Special Services.* Most publications offer a host of special services, including direct mail, merchandising assistance, ad reprints, and circulation audit reprints. You'll find the services offered by each publication listed in this section.

*Section 18: Circulation.* In addition to territorial distribution figures and a business anlaysis of the circulation, you will find the date the magazine was established as well as the single-copy and annual prices. The information in this section will be especially helpful when you are looking for magazines that reach the largest segments of your markets.

The information in SRDS is organized so that you can easily compare one publication with another. However, the additional material you will get when you ask the publishers for media kits will add considerable precision to your selection. These kits generally include the results of readership studies, more detailed circulation analysis, and market information that can be very helpful.

You may also find the *Business Press Cost Guide* helpful. It's a condensation of rate, circulation, and production data. For information on this guide, write to The Media Book, Inc., 75 East 55th Street, New York, NY 10022.

## HOW TO EVALUATE CIRCULATION

SRDS will give you the bare numbers. You will know, for example, that one publication has more readers than another, but this really isn't enough to make good decisions. You will want to know how many prospects might see your ad, and how the circulation base was built. You will want to know the circulation information and how well the publication is read. Let's look at circulation first.

The publisher's circulation statement is the best place to start your media review. Ideally, the statement will be verified by one of the independent auditing organizations. The two organizations that you will encounter most frequently are ABC and BPA.

ABC, the Audit Bureau of Circulations, is an organization sponsored by publishers, agencies, and advertisers to validate the circulation statements of paid-circulation publications. BPA, the Business Publications Audit of circulations, monitors business publications and is primarily concerned with controlled-circulation magazines. A third organization, the Verified Audit

Circulation Company, is a profit-making company that audits paid- and controlled-circulation publications.

There are a number of reasons to use the statements provided by one of the auditing services.

1. The services are impartial, and the information is provided in standardized form for easy evaluation and comparison.

2. When standardized information is presented, less time must be spent on details. The advertiser can concentrate on other assets, such as editorial strength and merchandising services that may be available.

3. Standardized audits protect the publisher—and the advertiser—from unfair comparisons.

4. Because of the reliability of independent audits, advertisers tend to use publications rated by the services more than those that are not audited. This tends to push unaudited publishers to put their circulation in shape for an audit—a decided benefit to the advertiser using the magazine.

The Media Comparability Council of the Business and Professional Advertising Association has developed a form designed to assist in the analysis of business and professional magazines by presenting information in a concise and orderly manner.

## What to Look for in an ABC Statement

ABC statements contain a lot of very helpful information, but it's easy to get bogged down if you don't know how to use them efficiently. These hints will be helpful, but they are no substitute for a thorough evaluation of all of the information.

Circulation figures are shown for a six-month period. The figures by themselves are not very meaningful, but when compared with the figures for the same period one year earlier, you can get a picture of growth or decline of the circulation.

When you use the same six-month periods, you will correct for any seasonal variations that could be misleading if you used two sequential statements.

When using the business/occupational analysis section, you can make comparisons with other ABC-audited publications serving the same field. However, the requirements for reporting by publications audited by BPA are different, so the information is not directly comparable.

One measure of the quality of a publication's circulation can be gleaned from a review of the subscription rate section. If you are comparing publications serving the same field, the magazine with the fewest subscriptions below the basic price is generally felt to have a higher-quality circulation.

If a magazine has to use special inducements to build its circulation, you should question the quality. Paragraph 8 of the ABC Statement shows how the circulation was built. If the circulation was built without the use of premiums, you can feel reasonably secure about the quality. However, when premiums are used, especially those that are not related to the nature of the publication, or those with a value close to the subscription price, the quality of the circulation should be questioned. Many publications use material reprinted from the pages of issues as subscription premiums. Generally speaking, when these are used to build circulation, there is little chance that the quality will be reduced as it is when unrelated premiums are used.

You should check to see how the subscription base was built. It's generally felt that subscriptions sold by direct order or by mail request reflect the highest-quality readership. The other sources of subscription sales are valuable, but not as much as those ordered directly. Some publications have requirements that must be met before an individual can have a subscription. Knowing the qualifications and how rigidly they are enforced can help when you are trying to decide among several publications. Some publications are sent to subscribers as part of an association membership. Such circulation is generally viewed as being lower in quality than direct subscribers because there is no evidence that the readers wanted the publication when they joined the association. They may value the subscription highly, but there is no way of knowing this from the data in the statement.

## What to Look for in a BPA Statement

Because most of the magazines audited by BPA are controlled, or nonpaid circulation publications, you will want to look closely at the sections that describe the readers. The introductory statement will give you an idea of the individuals and the types of businesses that are represented in the circulation. This is the publisher's general statement, and it is qualified in section 3a. The information in this section will help you to determine how many of the recipients are prospects for the products you plan to advertise.

Section 3b is especially important because it shows you where and how the magazine's circulation was built. The more readers who get the magazine as a result of a personal request, the better the quality of the circulation. In this table, you will also find a breakdown of the qualification time period. Magazines with the heaviest requalification circulation a year or less old will, in general, be better for your advertising. Turnover is so rapid in most industries that if a magazine has a large number of recipients that have not been requalified in several years, it could be ineffective.

Look carefully at section 3c. Here you will find how the copies are addressed. When most of the circulation is sent to individuals by name and title or function, the list will be a lot stronger than those that are sent out only by title or job function.

Section 4, the geographical breakdown, can be helpful in several ways. If you are selling nationally, you can determine if your distribution correlates with the audience. And, if you have regional distribution, you can determine how much of the audience will be of value and how much will be wasted.

The Verified Audit Circulation Corporation makes circulation audits for all publications, regardless of the field served, amount of paid circulation or manner of distribution.

## HOW TO EVALUATE READERSHIP

Some qualitative information can be gathered from the ABC and BPA statements, but neither will tell you anything about the quality of the editorial content. Your best media buys will reach the people you consider to be prime prospects and they will reach them with quality editorial content. It's relatively easy to compare circulation when you're evaluating media, but judging the editorial quality becomes a little sticky.

The first step is subjective; you should get about a half dozen back copies of each of the magazines you think might be valuable. Look at the articles that appear in each issue, and make a note of the regular features and columns. Is this the material that your prospects would read? Is it helpful? Current? Clearly written?

Check each publisher's editorial statement. You may find this in the media kit, but are sure to find it at the outset of the periodical's *Standard Rate and Data* listing. It's a good idea to check the statements made in this section with a review of the articles in the back copies you have received. Do the publishers' statements square with the actual editorial material?

Be sure to find out how the editorial material is generated. Some publications depend heavily on outside contributors, but the better magazines have good editorial control over contributed material. Others may print whatever is submitted to them with very little editorial review. It's important to know just how much control the editorial staff exercises over contributed material. A magazine with limited editorial control is often little more than a direct mail vehicle for advertisers. But one with a strong editorial department will have the support and respect of its readers. It's a good idea to check the qualifications of the editorial personnel, if you can. This information is seldom printed in any magazine promotional material unless the publisher is especially proud of the staff. You'll have to ask questions to get insight. The best editors are usually qualified in the field in which they work and have gained editorial skills by way of special education as well as on-the-job training.

Check to see if the magazine and its editors are quoted elsewhere—a sure sign of excellence. Has the magazine or its editors won any awards from the fields they serve as well as from the publishing industry?

Perhaps the most used and abused data comes from publication readership studies. No standard forms are used, such as those developed by the circulation auditing associations, and each readership study must be looked at from a different point of view. But, when they are well planned and carried out, readership studies can be very helpful.

You should always remember that readership studies are initiated by publishers to show the quality of their readership. Even if there is no out-and-out finagling, the goal of these studies is to present the magazine in the best possible light. Honest publishers will include any negative findings in their reports, but you will have to look to find them.

Studies conducted by publishers should be viewed more critically than those conducted by independent research organizations. However, even those done by independent organizations should be viewed with care. After all, the publisher did pay for the study and has a vested interest in the outcome.

You should know how the study was carried out. Direct interview studies are usually considered more reliable than those done by phone or through the mail. And be sure to note the date of the study. Readership changes so dramatically from year to year, that a six-month-old study may no longer reflect the views of the readers. You should also know where the study was conducted.

It's important to know something about the sampling techniques used. If the study was drawn on a statistically sound basis, you can rely more on it than if it was done with a few random phone calls. Studies done by independent consultants usually state the sampling conditions in the report.

It's just as important to know something about the design of the questionnaire and the interviewing method. You should look for questions that lead the respondents to certain conclusions as evidence of unsound design.

The data acquisition process may have been sound, but a lot of precision can be lost in the editing and tabulation process. See if the editing standards were objective, and not slanted to produce certain results. You can often spot a lack of objectivity by comparing the research done by two or more competitive magazines.

And, of course, it's important to determine if the conclusions are warranted from the data. Don't accept conclusions uncritically. Make the publisher support every statement with information drawn from the objective data.

## HOW TO EVALUATE THE ADVERTISING CARRIED IN A PUBLICATION

A number of different independent research organizations provide advertising research services for magazine publishers. Each has a different way of showing advertising effectiveness. Some will give readership scores, and others will break down this information into several components. These studies can be very helpful, but remember that each was paid for by the publisher who is using it to sell advertising. I have never known any of these studies to lie, but they can be used to emphasize the points the publisher wishes to make and avoid the points he wishes to hide.

You should check several issues to see how many of your competitors advertise in the magazines you are considering. Perhaps the best way to make use of this information is to see how many advertisers have been doing this for any length of time; if you pinpoint steady advertisers, you can be reasonably sure that the publication has been working for them. You can get information on the number of inquiries your competitors' ads have pulled by talking with the advertising representative. This is open information, but don't expect them to tell you who the respondents are.

## MANAGING A MEDIA PROGRAM

Once you have decided on the publications to be used and established the total space budget, you should plan the distribution of ads for a twelve-month period. Begin by scheduling all the special issues that you think will be of value. Some publishers list their special issues in S.R.D.S. However, all will provide you with an editorial schedule if you request it. If, for example, you make valves, you would want to be in the fluid control issue of an instrumentation magazine, if one were

Tek-Mark, Inc.
223 Old Hook Road/Westwood, New Jersey 07675

№ 501

☐ If checked here, this is an Insertion Order ☐ If checked here, this is a change or Cancellation Order

To the Publisher of: ______

Address: ______ City/State/Zip: ______

Attention: ______ Date: ______

Please Publish the Advertising of: ______

Division/Product: ______ Ad #: ______ Code: ______

SPACE TIMES DATES OF INSERTION

Position: ______ Headline: ______

Additional Instructions: ______

Rate: $ ______

Color: $ ______

Position: $ ______

Bleed: $ ______

TOTAL: $ ______

Send checking copies to:

Less agency commission of ______

Less cash discount of ______

Prepared by: ______
TEK-MARK, INC.

*NOTE: Please initial and date this acknowledgement and return to agency. If not initialed and returned within 14 days, the agency will assume that this insertion order is accepted by the publication.*

Accepted: ______ Date: ______

**Figure 7-1 An advertising insertion order**

After you have scheduled the issues that will be of special value, finish out the scheduling by placing space so that you get even coverage for the year. And don't worry about the summer in most cases. It has been shown that ad readership actually goes up in some industries during the summer. Avoid summer advertising only if your industry is seasonal and the summer is slow. This just isn't the case in most industrial markets. Despite vacations, trade magazine advertising is seen and acted on just as well in summer as in other months.

Your insertion order should carry the name of your house agency. And it should include all of the information shown on the form reproduced here. This form covers the most important points and provides for a checking system by requesting that the insertion order, or a copy of it, be returned initialed by the publisher.

Don't think that your job is done once you have set up the schedule and sent insertion orders. You must monitor the responses carefully after each ad has run. In general, forty-five to sixty days after the appearance of the ad is sufficient time to get a reading. Your first ad should provide a benchmark against which you can monitor its repeat appearance. In general, repeated ads will pull approximately the same number of inquiries each time they are run in a magazine for quite a while. The reason for this is simple. Not every issue is read, or even scanned by every subscriber so that each insertion has many new readers each time. However, watch the inquiries and when an ad starts to show signs of wear, pull it and replace it with another. Of course, if you have a multiproduct line you will probably run a number of different ads in succeeding issues.

Whatever you do, keep good records. Not only will the information help you evaluate your ads and the magazines in which you place them, it will also help you to keep tabs on market trends. A sudden spurt of interest in an advertised product could signal market changes that should be exploited.

## DIRECT-RESPONSE CARDS

Many magazines and independent publishers now produce and mail packets of direct-response cards. These cards contain ads for individual advertisers, and they are returned directly to the advertiser, not through the publisher as is done with magazine inquiries. Generally, they produce more leads for the same money spent on space ads. But many advertisers feel they are lower in quality.

These cards can be very effective ways to develop sales leads, but their success depends mainly on the quality of the mailing lists being used. The card packs produced by magazine publishers are sent to their circulation lists, so it is possible to evaluate the lists by checking their ABC or BPA statements. However, those produced by independent publishers must be checked carefully. Many of the independents will give you circulation information that is as carefully analyzed as that prepared for magazine circulation.

# Chapter 8

# Direct Mail Techniques that Work

Most business-to-business advertisers talk a lot about direct mail, but when the chips are down, the budgets usually get spent on ad space and trade shows. Have you ever wondered why? The answer is simple: It's a whole lot tougher to run a successful direct mail campaign than it is to handle a space program.

Very few companies have made waves in industrial direct mail—and for good reason. Traditionally, direct mail for consumer products is used to solicit cash directly. But how many industrial products can be sold at the usual consumer product price level, and how many prospects are there in even the largest industrial market?

To further complicate matters, most industrial advertising agencies look the other way when the client talks about direct mail. The 15 percent, plus creative fees for space advertising, can return a reasonable profit, but it's difficult to make money on a typical industrial direct mail campaign—unless, of course, it's handled on a fee basis. But, as you know, this arrangement is typically unpopular with most industrial advertisers.

The conventional industrial advertising agency not only lacks the financial motivation to undertake a direct mail program for its clients, it seldom has the expertise and experience. It's a whole new world, and unless the agency has direct mail copywriters, list managers, and production people who know how to keep costs down, a mail campaign can spin wheels and lose money quickly.

If all of this hasn't made you decide to move on to the next chapter without finishing this one, let me say that with some effort, and a little outside help if you aren't big enough to establish a full-fledged direct mail department, you can probably do more, dollar for dollar, than most of your competitors do with space. You may not get people to send you money through the mail, but you can do a lot to make those expensive personal sales calls more productive, and you might even find a way to sell your products through the mail. It's being done every day, but those who are doing it aren't likely to tell the world what has worked and what has bombed.

In that last sentence lies the real strength of direct mail. You can test a campaign, or any part of it, for very little money before you jump in with an expensive program. This is something that is very difficult to do with the usual small industrial advertising space budget. But, more about this later.

## DIRECT MAIL GOALS

Direct mail, like any other promotional method, can only succeed when you know what can be accomplished, and when you set specific goals. You can do a lot with direct mail, but there is a lot that can't be done. Here are some of the ways many successful industrial advertisers have found to use direct mail.

### Locate Prospects

Not everyone who uses your products will be a prospect at the moment you try to sell them. If you are selling expensive capital equipment, you may make a sale once every two or three years to a particular company. But you had better be there with your sales pitch when that prospect decides it's time to buy.

On the other hand, if you are selling a product that is consumed regularly by industry, such as hinges sold as O.E.M. products to builders of cabinets, your product is probably purchased regularly and on a predictable basis. The job of direct mail in this case is to sway the buyer from his or her present source. The job of the direct mail piece promoting the capital equipment is to snag the buyer when he or she is ready so that a sales call will be productive.

As you can see, it's important to understand the purchasing behavior of your market before you use direct mail to locate prospects. But once you understand the buying habits of your prospects, there are many direct mail techniques you can use to locate those who will be most receptive.

At certain times mailing a sample with the mailing piece can be effective. Of course, the product must be mailable and relatively inexpensive or the cost of the program will be quite high. However, if you mail to a small and select list, it's often practical to mail rather expensive samples. I once created a program for a client that involved sequentially mailing all of the components that were used to make a high-pressure needle valve. By itself, the valve was much more expensive than most products that are promoted by sampling. Each component was sent separately, and the mailings were done one week apart. A selling letter describing the benefits of each of the components was included in the mailings along with step-by-step instructions for the assembly of the valve. By the time each person got the final part, he or she not only had a complete valve, he or she had been exposed to a sales message nine times. Only 50 people were on this very select list and the campaign paid off very well.

Rather than send the sample outright, you can use your mailing to offer the sample. When those on your list write and request the sample, send it. Many advertisers who use this technique don't use post-paid forms for response. They specify that the request must be made on company letterhead. This tends to weed out the curiosity seekers and to identify those with a more serious interst in the product.

Some advertisers have found that the offer of a demonstration is a very effective way to locate prospects. Usually the people who respond are serious, and seldom willing to waste their time and the time of the person who stages the demonstration.

## Enhancing a Sales Call

Many products and services sold to business users require considerable explanation. With the cost of an average sales call now well over $100, anything that can make these calls more effective should be tried. Precall mailings that set the stage for the call and relate much of the product detail that would have to be explained during the visit will help salespeople make more effective calls.

Follow-up mailings can be used to continue the momentum of a sales call. Astute salespeople can usually pick up on the problems their prospects have that relate to their products. Letters aimed specifically at these questions can greatly enhance the effectiveness of a call.

It's bothersome and time-consuming to have to create a new letter for each call. Because most people tend to have similar interests and ask essentially the same questions, many companies have developed letter books of standard paragraphs. When a follow-up letter is required, the salesperson simply gives the numbers of the appropriate paragraphs to his or her secretary and the letter is done in minutes. If needed, a personalized paragraph can be added, but the main points of the letter are taken care of quickly and effectively.

## Selling Products by Mail

As I mentioned earlier, not many business-to-business advertisers sell products directly through the mail. However, certain products lend themselves well to mail selling, and when promoted properly, people will order and reorder regularly. The best products sold by mail are usually relatively inexpensive, and can be reordered on a regular basis.

In fact, most mail order businesses, whether they are selling to industry or to consumers, look to build repeat sales. They often make little or no money on the first sale just to get the account opened. However, once regular buying habits have been established, it's difficult to get satisfied customers to buy any other way.

What products can be sold this way? Many maintenance products, such as roofing compounds and cleaning agents have been sold successfully through the mail. Small OEM products such as resistors, nails, and hardware have been sold well through the mail. One very successful company markets cleaning chemicals and tools strictly to the computer trade. The products are small, easy to ship, not breakable, and expendable—all characteristics that help insure a successful direct mail operation.

## Bring Prospects to You

You can use direct mail to invite prospects to your plant, or to see your products displayed at regional distribution points. And you can use it quite effectively to get people to visit your booth at a trade show.

## Gather Information

Direct mail market research won't result in orders, but it is one of the best ways to gather information. You can, with a letter, questionnaire, and a post-paid envelope, ask questions of your prospects, customers, dealers, and sales force. However, don't try to sell in a research letter. In fact, you should try very hard to impress your readers that you are seeking only their views, not their orders. The best way to do this is to tell them NOT to sign the questionnaire because knowing their name would invalidate the sample. This isn't true, but it does create a feeling of confidence, and will let the recipient feel that you won't bound back with an order pad once he or she has responded.

## Institutional Advertising

There are times when it's important to tell people just how marvelous you are. Don't brag and boast to the point of turning off your reader, but do tell your story in terms of benefits. See the chapter on copywriting for some hints on how to handle this.

## HOW TO JUDGE RESULTS

Folklore abounds in this business about the percentage of inquiries one should expect from a mailing, depending on all sorts of conditions. It's true that slight changes in seemingly insignificant elements of a mailing campaign can turn a loser into a winner, but to bank on any percentages at all is a mistake. In the mail order publishing business, marketing managers are fond of saying, "You don't bank percentages, you bank money." This is true in any direct mail operation. I've seen businesses make a good profit with less than a 1 percent response and others fold up with a response of over 5 percent to their mailings.

Most business-to-business advertisers won't be reading this chapter to try to enter the mail order business; they will be seeking ways to use direct mail to augment their existing sales force. Therefore, the following simple system of direct mail evaluation should be quite helpful.

There is no way of knowing in advance just how successful any mailing campaign will be. However, every company that succeeds in direct mail does so because it keeps meticulous records of its successes and failures as well as the reasons for each. Out of this research will come guidelines that can help shape future mailings. Here's a typical case.

1. The Ace Company found that one out of twenty direct mail leads turns into a sale, and the average sale is $2,000.

2. By dividing the average sale by twenty, they found that each inquiry is worth $100.

3. Assume the annual sales quota is $2,000,000. When you divide this figure by the value of an inquiry, you will see that 20,000 inquiries are needed to meet the quota.

4. Further, assume that the average response to the company's mailings is 4 percent.

5. Therefore, 500,000 pieces must be mailed in the year.

Mailing 500,000 pieces doesn't mean that the company will have to find 500,000 unduplicated names to mail to. Rather, it means that they must select lists carefully that have been successful in the past and mail to them several times during the year. Simply because you have mailed to a company or an individual and they didn't respond the first time doesn't mean that they won't respond the next time they get your mailing. In fact, research has shown that productive lists can be used over and over again with the same offer, and will generally pull about the same response each time. Of course, smart mail order people who do this watch the productivity of their lists very carefully. When the response begins to fade, they drop the list. Oddly enough, just letting a previously successful list lie fallow for a period is often enough to revive it for future mailings. However, there is no fixed criterion for this, and every advertiser must determine his or her own limits strictly by experience.

## MAILING LISTS

Although I cut my advertising teeth as a copywriter and feel very strongly about the importance of copy in the success of a campaign, the most critical element of a mail campaign will always be the list. The difference between good and poor copy may be less than a percent in terms of responses, but the difference between good and bad lists is almost always the difference between profit and loss.

The best mailing list you will ever have will be made up of the names and addresses of your present customers. Most companies can do more to increase their bottom line by using direct mail to increase purchases by present customers than by most other methods. The next best list will be made up of the people who have responded to your space advertising and product publicity, and of visitors to your trade show exhibits. And, of course, the names given you by your sales people will be strong. If you use reps or distributors, urge them to give you the names of their customers and prospects. However, these names are their lifeblood and some of them will never part with their lists. You can use them, though, if the distributors will agree to make the mailing for you, rather than to turn over their lists for your use. When this is done, it's customary to pay all expenses, including the services to run the list and do the mailing.

You can also build a list by using published directories in your field and the names of trade show registrants, as well as business sections of telephone directories and membership rolls of associations that serve your field. However, these are secondary sources and not likely to be as effective as the sources I outlined in the previous paragraph.

## Using Someone Else's Mailing List

There is a thriving trade in the use of other company's mailing lists, and you can get them directly or through the services of a mailing list broker. Brokers act as middlemen, putting the advertiser together with the list owner for a fee. The brokerage fee is paid by the list owner, for whom the broker works. It's also possible to rent lists from publishers of trade magazines in your field as well as directly from the owners of lists.

Whatever way you secure your lists, the chances are that you will seldom have them in hand—you will be given the use of the list only. That is, you will send the material you want to mail to the letter shop that manages the list and they will handle the entire operation, without letting the list go out of their building. Mailing lists are valuable properties, and it's no trick to have one duplicated. Therefore, most lists are rented for one-time use only, and the processing is done by an agent of the list owner.

However, some companies will send you a copy of their list, and will specify for one-time use only. Don't think you can get away with duplicating the list and using it again. Most list owners who give you a hard copy of their list salt it with a name and address you would never recognize, and use this name to check on usage. Use the list for a second mailing, and they'll send you a bill and will have the right to collect.

## List Selectivity

Whether you buy, rent, or swap lists, you can get names and addresses of just about anything and anyone in any way you want them. You can make very broad selections by using two-digit SIC (Standard Industrial Classification) numbers, and you can refine this selection by job titles or functions and even by specific geographic locations. The ZIP codes have made it possible for users of the mail to target areas right where they have representation.

Many compiled lists are available by title only. That is, you may be interested in hospital microbiologists and rent a list that is slugged "Microbiologist, such-and-such hospital." These lists do work, but you are usually better off buying a list with the name of the individual who is the microbiologist at such-and-such hospital. However, as your requirements become more specific, the costs will go up. Generally speaking, if you're selling expensive equipment, you should look for lists that are specific—by name, title, job function, location, etc. However, if you're trying to get broad exposure for your product, less selective lists may be the better choice.

Of course, the ultimate is the fill-in letter in which the name of the individual is actually typed on the letter by computer-controlled equipment. This, of course, is very expensive. But, where exclusivity and impact are important, this technique does pay off.

## How to Rent a List

If the list you want to use is a big one, you should test a portion of it before you commit to the total mailing. This is standard practice, but the amount used for the test will vary from list to list. Usually the list owner will specify a minimum that can be used for the test. Unless you want to test the viability of a specific portion of the list, you should specify a random, or an nth, name sample. If, for example, the list that interests you has 100,000 names, and the owner specifies that a minimum test will be 10 percent, an nth name test sample will be every tenth name. You may not want to mail to this sample again if the test is successful, and it's usually possible to eliminate the test names from the balance of the list.

Rates are quoted net to the mailer; however, advertising agencies (including house agencies) are usually allowed a commission. Mailing list brokers are given a 20 percent commission by the list owner.

Before ordering a list, make sure you know what kind of equipment your letter shop has for affixing the labels. There are a number of systems, and unless the list is prepared for the equipment that will be used, it will be useless.

Perhaps the most complete source of mailing lists available for rent is *Standard Rate and Data Services Direct Mail Directory*. See the Appendix for the SRDS address, as well as for addresses of other direct mail sources.

## How to Select the Best Rental List

Most owners who rent their lists regularly will provide you with a card that contains all of the specifications needed to make a good selection. Check your criteria against the data on these cards and pick only those that fit most closely. When the lists you review seem to be less than the best matches, test them carefully first.

If you feel that the list is going to work for you, you should think about getting duplicate copies, or ordering duplicate runs in the first order for future mailings. It's less expensive to order several uses at once than it is to order individual runs.

If you can, try to find out how the list is maintained, and how often it is brought up to date. If the list is used regularly for first-class mailings, the nondeliverable mail should have been returned to the list owner and he or she should have removed the names from the list. If the list has had infrequent use, you should ask the owner why and determine whether the owner has mailed to it for the purposes of updating. Old names are of little value. Some direct mail people estimate that every month 2 percent of most lists go sour for one reason or another. That's a big 24 percent a year. Think of this in terms of wasted printing, postage and sales!

Be sure that the list is in ZIP code sequence to insure rapid delivery.

If you're going to test a portion of the list, make sure that the samples are representative of the entire list. This is a tough order, and some list owners have been accused of salting their samples with the hot names on their lists to make the rental of the entire list more appealing.

You should try to find out who else has used the list. It's a good idea to talk with other users to get an idea of how successful the list has been for them. When you do this, be sure you find out what the product was and how it was offered. If a previous user rented the list to offer a free catalog, a high response is to be expected. However, if the list was used to sell a product directly, the percentages will be way down scale.

## HOW TO KEEP YOUR MAILING LIST UP TO DATE

When you start building your own mailing list, don't assume that the people on it will be prospects forever. People move to new companies, move up in their present companies, die, retire, and go on to other assignments where they no longer have a need for your products. If your mailings are going to be cost effective, you have to keep your list up to date at all times.

Even before you face the problems of maintaining a list, you should be sure that the names are accurate when they are first added. Be sure to spell everyone's name correctly, and if they have titles, make sure that they are accurate.

If many of the people on your list are employed by large companies, it pays to check the address carefully to make sure that the mail is being routed to the correct department. A lot of Smiths work for IBM. If you want to reach a specific Smith, you had better know exactly where your Smith is in the company.

In the beginning, you will probably keep your list on one of the smaller duplicating type of addressing systems. This equipment is very practical for lists of several thousand names, but beyond this, you should consider the possibility of using either your own or someone else's data processing equipment. I mention this at this point only because you will have to tailor your list-keeping activities to meet the demands of the system you use. Duplicator-type addressing machines use paper plates that print in the same way as a spirit duplicator. Changes in the names on lists maintained this way usually require that the old paper plate be destroyed and a new one made. The same is true of metal plate addressing equipment, such as the Addressograph. More on equipment later.

A list should be kept up to date. This will be an automatic procedure if you mail to the list regularly. When your mailings are sporadic, you may have to mail specifically for the purpose of cleaning the list. You may want to handle the list maintenance yourself if you have the people, time, and equipment. But, as your list grows in size and complexity, you will probably opt for the use of an outside organization that will not only handle all your mailings, but also handle all of the list maintenance functions.

It's often best to start a list-cleaning operation with your sales force. Most companies will have the list run for each sales territory and ask their salespeople to check it and return with comments. This is an excellent way to keep a list up to date. Not only will the local salespeople be able to nix those who should no longer be on the list, they should be able to provide new names for your list.

However, this is a time-consuming activity, and it could turn out to be expensive in terms of reduced sales activity during the time the salespeople are working on the list. But, you can often have the best of two worlds by giving the salespeople plenty of time to do the job. When they can do it as a fill-in, it will be best for all concerned.

Some companies have offered their salespeople special bonuses for list-cleaning work. Some pay for each name added or cleaned, and others have run contests offering prizes for the work.

One of the most successful ways to clean a list is a direct approach: Ask those on the list whether they still want to receive material from you. However, this job must be handled with care. If you're not a direct mail copywriter, I strongly suggest that you use a good free-lancer for the job. With all the adverse publicity that has appeared recently about junkmail, you need a good copy touch in your list-cleaning letter, or you may find yourself with no list at all.

The pros in the field all seem to agree that the light approach works best. This appears to be true for just about every type of person to whom you might be mailing, whether they are very sophisticated scientists, or nuts and bolts mechanics.

When you make a list-purge mailing, you will probably have to mail to the list two or three times before you can be sure that you have gotten everyone who should remain on your list. Every mailing will miss some people, and some of those who saw the first or second letter might not respond until they see your third request.

Making purge mailings can be expensive, especially if you created the mailing solely for the purpose of cleaning your lists. However, if you establish a program of regular list maintenance, the cost will be less, and your list will be more current than if you make only periodic stabs at it. The mainstay of a regular list-cleaning program should be internal. That is, you should have your salespeople, inside and outside, submit changes and additions. Beyond that there are a number of ways to have the post office help.

Depending on how you mail, you can use the post office offers to help you keep your list clean. Some of them might seem expensive, but you will find it more expensive to print and mail to people who are no longer prospects. Here are the services that are most practical and helpful for the business mailer to use to keep a list current. The post office charges fees for its services. Rather than list the costs as of the time of printing this book, I suggest that you check for current rates.

*Return postage guaranteed.* When this line is printed on the envelope of your mailing piece, the post office will, for a fee, return all undeliverable mail. The service varies with each mail classification, but it's a good way to discover who is no longer at the old address.

*Forwarding and return postage guaranteed.* This service is not available for first- and second-class mail, but it can be used for third- and fourth-class. The mail will be forwarded out of town at the applicable rate, and the sender must guarantee to pay forwarding and return postage if the addressee refuses to accept the mail. It is forwarded locally at no charge.

*Address correction requested.* When this line is printed on your envelope, first-class mail will be forwarded to the addressee's new address, and the post office will send a form to the sender with the old and new address. A fee is charged, but this service will help you keep track of your prospects. It's available for all other classes of mail.

*No marking on envelope.* When nothing is printed on an envelope used for first-class mail, undeliverable letters will be returned at no charge. This does not include post cards. The post office will forward the mail at no charge when the new address is on file. For other classes, unless the piece has obvious value, the post office will treat it as waste.

There are other classifications as well as specific circumstances for individual classes of mail, but this summary covers most of the situations relevant to business direct mail advertisers. If you are handling a lot of second-, third-, and fourth-class mail, it's wise to either talk with your postmaster, or try to get a copy of the rules governing forwarding, return, and address correction services.


## HOW TO SELECT A DIRECT MAIL FORMAT

A direct mail assignment gives the advertising person more creative latitude than any other medium. However, you must be careful not to try to be creative just to be different. Your creative efforts should all be directed toward a specific marketing goal. That goal may be direct sales, inquiries, or the enhancement of the corporate image, but you must never lose sight of the goal just to be clever.

All advertising, whether it's direct mail or space, should operate on the reader on two levels. Even though most industrial products have little to use in a psychological appeal, it's important to keep the reader's personal needs in mind as well as his or her business requirements. You may appeal to an economic motive by telling the reader that your springs hold their tension longer and therefore they will enhance the value of the product in which they are incorporated. But you shouldn't miss the opportunity to imply that the reader can be a hero when your products are chosen and they perform as specified. Used subtly, and coupled with a sound benefit, your copy will be more effective if you appeal to a personal benefit than if you deal only with the economic level.

You can use considerably longer copy in direct mail than you can in space advertising. Therefore, a number of formats are practical. But, which format will be most effective? This question cannot be answered in a vacuum; it must be considered in relation to the work the direct mail is expected to do. If the goals are immediate, such as the development of sales or inquiries by return mail, the format will be different from that which would be used to accomplish long-range corporate goals. The format should tell the reader what to expect. Because most businessmen have been exposed to considerable professionally prepared direct mail, they are conditioned to expect different pitches from different formats.

These are some of the formats that are most often used in business-to-business direct mail advertising.

## The Letter

The letter is the most widely used direct mail format, mainly because it is generally used in combination with other forms. It's also one of the most deceptively difficult pieces of advertising copy to write. Most executives are accustomed to writing many letters a day, and feel because of this that they can write a good sales letter. You may be one of the few who can, but writing good direct mail copy is one of the most demanding writing jobs in the advertising business. Good direct mail letters are fun to read, even if you have no interest in the product being promoted. It's because of this that most people think it's easy to write them. I know that the purpose of this book is to show you how to run your own in house agency, but if you plan to include an active direct mail program, either hire a full-time direct mail copywriter, or buy the free-lance services of a professional.

The letter is the most personal form of direct mail and it usually has the most impact. Letters can be hand-typed for distribution to a few target accounts or they can be reproduced by the thousands on printing presses. Modern data processing equipment has made it possible to create automatically typed letters that have the recipient's name and address, as well as a personal salutation, typed in so that it's all but impossible to detect that the letter wasn't hand-typed.

It's a good idea to begin a letter file now. That is, save all of the sales letters you receive and the material that is sent along with them. You will want to keep the good letters with the bad so you can easily see the contrasts. Become a reader of direct mail—don't discard anything without reading it. After a few weeks of this, you will begin to see patterns of copy style emerge, and this will help you when you write copy, or evaluate the copy written for you by professionals.

## The Folder

A folder is a small printed piece that is unbound. Folders generally run from an 8½ × 11 inch sheet folded to an appropriate envelope to an 11 × 17 inch sheet folded to 8½ × 11 inches or smaller. Folders are generally used to promote a single product, product line, or concept. They can be mailed in envelopes with letters or they can be used as self-mailers. If you go to the self-mailer route, be sure to select a paper with sufficient strength to travel. Generally speaking, a 70- or 80-pound text sheet will give you the strength you need.

## The Catalog

Catalogs can be used in a number of selling situations. When they are sent through the mail to people who are identified prospects they are generally filed and used when needed. Other types of direct mail are seldom kept.

Catalogs are used by companies that sell products through the mail as well as by people who make equipment that must be engineered for individual applications and that is sold for millions of dollars. In a sense, a catalog can serve as a showcase, a permanent record of the products and services offered by your company.

Plan your catalogs carefully. Write the copy in the language of the prospect who will read the catalog, and be sure to include all details. Remember, you can get into considerable detail in catalog copy. It's not like space advertising copy where you have to fight for attention as the reader is exposed to other ads as well as the editorial content. The prospect is already interested and wants details.

Make your catalogs easy to read and easy to use. If some of your products have features in common, it's tempting to list these features together, and then describe the individual features in separate sections. This is a big mistake. Even though you may have a lot of redundancy, each product should be presented completely and separately. No one wants to thumb back and forth between pages to get a full picture of the product in which they are interested.

## Brochures and Booklets

These mailing pieces are generally formed by binding several sections together. The binding can be a staple, glue, or stitching. Booklets are generally felt to create more of a "class" impression than the broadside or folder, even though each may have the same amount of image area. Booklets are often used when considerable copy is required. The amount of text on each page is less than would appear on a panel of a folder, and is, therefore, less imposing.

## House Organs and Newsletters

House organs are used for soft sell of the corporate image as well as for hard sell in which a direct order is solicited. Newsletters that provide real news and help for the reader can be very effective selling tools. Newsletters and company magazines that use case histories based on the use of the advertiser's products and services always rate high in effectiveness. However, they are not easy to do. It's very easy to lapse into a straight sales pitch as the story is written. Those who read these newsletters recognize that the purpose of the mailing is to sell, but if the sell in case history copy is kept to a minimum, a lot of information can be given to the reader.

## Gimmicks

Some very clever people have created some extremely effective direct mail with unusual gimmicks. Gimmicks range from unusual die cuts that pop up when the mailing piece is opened to slide calculators for specific applications and unusual ways of mailing samples. As I mentioned earlier, don't let a wild creative idea get in the way of selling. This doesn't mean that you should look for the tried and true, it means that you should start with a goal and then try to come up with a creative gimmick that will accomplish the goal, not just look flashy.

## Combinations

When you think of direct mail, don't start with a format. Start with the objective, and then decide on the format that will be most effective. More often than not, you will find that modifications and combinations of standard formats will be best. Be flexible—try several formats.

## DIRECT MAIL EQUIPMENT

The decision to do everything in-house means that you will have to select a system and equipment that will be most effective for your operation. Even though there is a lot of glamour in computer systems, if you have no data processing equipment that can be used to handle the mailing, you should investigate some of the conventional paper- and metal-plate systems. Most industrial mailing lists are relatively small, when compared with consumer direct mail lists. And most industrial lists are simple, in the sense that a lot of categories and break-outs are seldom required.

If you're going to operate your mailing services inside, you will also want to make sure that you have the people who can handle it. The people needed to handle lists and mailings should be very detail conscious. It seldom works out to have the work done by employees who have other assignments, unless your list is small and you don't plan to make many mailings.

I have found it's usually advisable to use an outside lettershop to handle these details. After all, you're probably not in the direct mail business, and are using direct mail as only a part of your total promotion program. An outside house doesn't add to the overhead, doesn't sit around costing you money when there is no work to do, and they know their business better than you will ever know it.

## WHAT CLASS OF POSTAGE TO USE

First-class mail with a hand-affixed stamp generally gets more attention than any other type of mail, except special delivery. However, if you use special delivery make sure that you have a good reason, other than to attract attention. Perhaps you have a timed offer, and special delivery will get it to the reader in time.

First-class mail applied with a postage meter will get almost the attention of a hand-affixed stamp, but when you get into third-class and bulk mailings, effectiveness begins to soften. However, as I mentioned several times, you must plan all aspects of a mailing campaign to achieve a goal. And the selection of the type of postal handling is included in this decision.

First class is delivered most quickly. Third class and bulk mail are delivered after all the first class has been delivered. If timing is not important, and you must reach a large audience, you will probably use bulk mail.

If you're going to mail first class with hand-affixed stamps, you should consider buying special issues to attract attention, rather than using the regular flag stamp.

## TECHNIQUES FOR MORE SUCCESSFUL DIRECT MAILINGS

There are no magic secrets that, when applied to any direct mail campaign, will guarantee success. However, some things have proved effective for so many mailers that it pays to consider them.

1. Get the selling off to a running start by using the envelope. Short copy on the envelope can turn mail that might have been junked without being read into a successful campaign. Most successful direct mail companies prefer to use teaser copy on the envelope, rather than give away the strength of the offer before the letter is read. We used a line that read "Corrosive material inside" to get people to open a letter that offered a special chart for

those using valves made of various metals used on corrosive service and in corrosive atmospheres. The envelope copy was tested against an envelope that had no copy. The keyed reply cards showed that the envelope copy more than doubled our response.

2. Give the reader something of value. If you don't want to include your new $5 catalog with every letter, you should offer it to those who send for it. And don't make it too difficult for them to respond. Enclose either a business reply card or envelope and, if possible, have the offer card preprinted with the respondent's name and address. This can be handled when the addressing is done on the response card and it is positioned in a window envelope for mailing.

3. Get the reader's attention immediately. Even though you can use long copy successfully in direct mail, the reader must be with you from the start or he or she will never get to your sales message. But, when you try for attention, be sure that the device you use relates to the rest of the copy, the product, and the offer. A flashy attention-getter that is not related to your product will stop the reader and will insure that the next mailer isn't even opened.

4. Test your copy, headline, and offer before you launch a full-blown campaign. But be sure to test only one element at a time. If you vary two elements in a letter, you will never know what is causing any differences in response. You can do all of your testing at one time, but be sure that each test piece is mailed to a different segment of your mailing list and that the reply cards are keyed so you can make a judgment.

5. Make sure that the reader is told or asked to do something specific when he or she is finished reading your direct mail piece. If you want the reader to send an order, say so. Don't beat around the bush. The copy should build to the point where specific action is required.

6. Plan your catalog so that the high-volume products are up front and prominently displayed. The big mail order people have their cataloging so finely tuned that they can usually predict the number of products that will be sold and the sales volume by the amount of space allocated and the position it occupies in the catalog.

7. Repeat your successful direct mail. If your mail works well, you can often use it again with the same list, as long as you let a little time go by. However, this obviously doesn't apply to timed material, such as a dated newsletter or company magazine.

# Chapter 9

# How to Create Your Own Publicity and Get It Published

You've spent a bundle on space advertising, but when you look at the hundreds, or possibly thousands of inquiries you receive from product publicity, you get the feeling that this "free advertising" is the only way to go. Right? Wrong!

In the first place, it isn't free. Second, it's not advertising. But it is the way to go if you plan and integrate it carefully with your space advertising program.

Just to set the record straight, here's how most professionals define advertising and publicity:

*Advertising.* The paid presentation or promotion of ideas, products, or services by an identified sponsor.

*Publicity.* A story or message about a product, idea, or service prepared as editorial material rather than as advertising, and published without cost.

The last two words in the definition of publicity are deceptive. It's true that the magazines don't charge for publicity as they do when they run an advertisement, but publicity isn't free. It's really rather expensive—but worth every penny. Here's a conservative estimate of the cost to prepare and mail 50 copies of a single-page release, as of 1980.

| | |
|---|---:|
| Writing | $150.00 |
| Stenography | 50.00 |
| Photography | 75.00 |
| Photoprints | 35.00 |
| Printing | 25.00 |
| Postage | 7.50 |
| Envelopes | 5.00 |
| Total cost | $347.50 |

If you've planned your publicity program carefully, you will have a release scheduled to mail every month. This brings your annual publicity budget up to $4,170.50. To most industrial advertisers, this is a trifle. But for the smaller advertiser who has a space budget that hovers around this figure, it's a lot of money. But this isn't the end. If you are careful about all your costs, you will account for the time spent by those who help prepare the releases: engineers, draftspeople, the shop people who polish the product for photography, and the endless number of individuals who will be asked to read and comment on the copy. For all this, you can add another $300 per release.

Now, how free is free publicity?

My main reason for this exercise is to intimidate you a little. I really want you to take publicity seriously. Unfortunately, when something appears to be free, we tend to take it lightly. But when we have to pay for something, it gets more attention. Publicity is one of the most cost-effective marketing communications tools you have. But there are a lot of pitfalls along the road to publication. Before I get into the nuts and bolts of developing publicity, I'd like to show you how to avoid the biggest of these pitfalls, failing to realize that publicity is most effective when it's part of an integrated marketing communications program.

## HOW TO BUILD STRONG EDITORIAL RELATIONS

Most editors of business, professional, and trade magazines take their work very seriously. If your release will interest, inform, and educate their readers, they will do everything they can to see that it gets into print. Even if you try to build your business solely on releases with no paid advertising, the best of these editors will still insist on editorial integrity and run your material. But the trade press survives on advertising revenue, and sooner or later you will find yourself shut out of the editorial pages. This isn't a hold-up. If your product is of sufficient interest to the readers of the editorial pages, it should have the same value when read as paid advertising. Take my advice and don't push the editors to this point. Not only is it bad for future relations, but it shows that you are either a cheapskate, or a person who has no idea of how an integrated marketing communications program should be put together.

Fortunately, editors and industrial public relations people have been working at this business long enough so that a set of guidelines has emerged that can help you considerably. Don't think that these are the guaranteed keys to publication: They're only the rules that most people have agreed to play by. If your product is of little interest and you have written a ho-hum release, there is very little you can do to get your story told. But if you have information of value to readers of the publications on your list, and play by these rules, your chances of publication will be good.

1. *Know the editors.*

Get to know the editors who are doing the most for the readers you want to reach. This means that you should know which publications are being read by those to whom you want to sell your products. There is hardly a field in science, industry, and business that isn't served by several publications. For some the number is small; for others, it's large. There are 318 magazines published for those in the health care and medical research fields. On

the other hand, there are only two magazines in the brick
and tile field.

Look at the masthead of the magazines you have
selected. Find the names of the editors who have responsibility for your field of interest. Some magazines are so
small that one editor does it all, but others may have
many editors in the staff. It's important to determine just
who it is you want to reach. You may be able to tell by
looking at job titles. If, for example, a publication lists a
new products editor, this is the person to whom you
would send your new-product releases. However, this
may not be the person to whom you would speak if you
wanted to place a feature article.

You should get to know each of these editors
personally. You may never meet face to face. But through
correspondence and phone conversations, you should get
to know each one. If you're just building your publicity
list, I suggest that you take the time to phone each of the
editors you have selected and introduce yourself. Tell
each what will be forthcoming. In some cases, you may
find that one or more of these editors has special issues
coming up that will be ideal for your product and will
suggest your sending a color transparency rather than the
conventional black and white print.

Once you have spoken with each of the editors, be
sure to follow up with a letter. Conscientious editors keep
a file of information sources just as you will keep a list of
editors to whom you will send your material.

2. *Know the publications.*

Develop an intimate knowledge of the publications
that serve your market. Every magazine has its own
editorial format and needs. When you know what has
been published in the past, you will know how to
approach your task of placing publicity. This point is
especially important when you are trying to place a
feature story on an exclusive basis. However, when you
are sending publicity releases to all of the magazines on

your list, it is all but impossible to write each release to suit the publications you have chosen. Once you have highlighted the characteristics of each publication in a field, you will probably come up with several elements that hang together and can be played upon when writing publicity for general distribution.

Write to the editor of each of the magazines you have selected and ask for an editorial schedule. Most publications plan their editorial calendar a year in advance. With this information you can spot your releases and feature materials in the issues that will do the most good. I have found it helpful to make up a composite calendar of special editorial issues for each client for all of the important publications. With such a schedule, you can tell at a glance what's coming up, and plan for coverage. A word of caution, though. Product publicity in special issues should be sent out at least three months in advance and preferably four months ahead of the date of the issue—marked very clearly that you would prefer it to be in the special issue. And you should contact an editor at least six months ahead of the date of a special issue if you would like to try for the placement of a feature story. If you are unsure of all of the publications that serve your markets, you can get the information from a copy of the *Standard Rate and Data Service* directory. As mentioned earlier, this guide is published monthly and sold to advertisers and agencies. You may find copies in larger local libraries. In this directory you will also find most of the information you will need to make preliminary media selection for advertising. *Bacon's Publicity Checker* is also very helpful, and less expensive than SRDS. However, Bacon's is limited to information that will help you only place publicity. There is no rate and advertising information. (Publisher information for both books is given in the Appendix.)

No matter how much information you get from directories, there is no substitute for first-hand knowledge of the magazines you will be using. Once you know which you think will be important, I suggest that you contact each and ask them to send you a media file as well as a few recent issues. Study these issues for the editors' needs and to see if any will require special treatment of your releases.

3. *Take the editors into your confidence.*

Don't spring surprises on the editors and expect them to respond with enthusiasm at the last minute no matter how well you know them. If you have something coming up that you feel requires more attention than just a straight product publicity release, talk with the editors you feel are best for the project.

4. *Give each magazine a shot at an exclusive.*

To anyone who has had bad luck placing material in the trade press, this may sound unusual, but try to spread your specials around so that many of the magazines covering your field get occasional exclusives. Of course, if there is one magazine that dominates all others by a wide margin, then try to stick with the winner.

5. *Don't use advertising for leverage.*

Whatever you do, don't pressure an editor with the promise of an ad if your material is run. Not only is it very unprofessional, but it can result in closed doors at the publications that may be best able to help you. More often than not, any pressure on an editor will be reported to others on the magazine. Even though the magazine lives by advertising revenue, you will have a tough time getting anything published, regardless of how much you advertise. And don't use current advertising to apply pressure, either.

6. *Invite editors to your plant.*

If it's convenient, invite the editors you would like to work with to visit your plant. But when you do, be sure that you have something important for them at the time of the visit.

7. *One magazine per exclusive.*

Don't place the same feature story in two or more competitive publications. Of course, this doesn't apply to general product and news releases. When an editor commits the pages of his or her magazine to your article, it's for exclusive publication. There's no faster way to lose an editorial friend than to pull this stunt. And don't think that even a major revision of the same material will get you off the hook. One story, one publication.

8. *Accept an editor's rejection gracefully.*

If an editor turns you down, don't go over his or her head. Talk it over with the editor and find out why, but don't run to the editor's boss with your tale. In most cases, the editor can give you sound reasons why the material wasn't used. If the editor is doing his or her job, and the decision didn't involve anything personal, the boss will back up the decision.

## HOW TO BUILD YOUR PUBLICITY LIST

Beg, borrow, or buy a copy of the business publication edition of *Standard Rate and Data Service.* If your library doesn't have a copy, you might be able to get a back issue from a local advertising agency. SRDS is published monthly, and it's important for agencies to have a frequent update for rate and circulation information. But for your publicity purposes, a copy several months old will be fine. However, if you're really serious about your house agency, you should subscribe. Write to Standard Rate and Data Service, 5201 Old Orchard Road, Skokie, IL 60077, for the current subscription price.

You can spend less money for a copy of *Bacon's Publicity Checker.* It will be just as helpful for publicity, but it has no information to help you make advertising decisions. For the price of the current edition, write to Bacon's Publishing Company, 14 East Jackson Boulevard, Chicago, IL 60604. Bacon's will tell you the kind of publicity each publication will accept, something you will have to guess at when you use SRDS. If you're serious about a house agency, you should have both.

Let's assume that you have a copy of SRDS. The first step in using the directory is to turn to the Classification Grouping section, a table of contents arranged according to specializations. Within each grouping you will find listed the publications that serve the field. Don't stop once you have found the category that seems to be most important to you. Look at each category to see if there aren't any peripheral classifications that could be important.

For example, suppose that you make flow meters, and find that Section 34: Controls and Instrumentation Systems lists the publications you feel are most important. You will probably have the prime magazines in this section, but look what you might be missing if you stopped there:

Section 6: Automotive. Your flow meter might be usable on engine test stands.

Section 7: Aviation and Aerospace. Consider all the gases and liquids that must be measured and controlled in this field.

Section 15A: Bottling. What about the dispensing applications where flow meters act as the control?

Section 16: Brewing. Flow measurement is critical, not only for the processing applications, but for government-mandated measurement for tax purposes.

Section 28: Chemical Processing. The applications in this field probably outnumber those that might be reached with publicity in the instrument publications.

Section 40B: Energy Application. Flow measurement plays a part in fuel system planning as well as with liquid coolants.

Section 70: Industrial Distribution. The advertiser might want to expose the flow meter to industrial distributors.

Section 111: Petroleum and Oil. Flow meters are used in extraction as well as processing applications.

Section 115B: Pollution Control. Most of the liquid and gas pollution control standards require careful measurement of effluent flow.

Section 155: Water and Sewage Disposal. Again, the applications for a flow meter are obvious.

Thirteen publications are listed in what you might have thought to be the main section—Controls and Instrumentation Systems. However, without too much imagination, you can see applications in each of the other fields. There are more than 150 publications in these sections that should receive your release.

Now that you have picked the sections that will be valuable, you will have to check out the publications described in each. For publicity purposes, you can skip over the material that will only be of interest when you are planning an advertising schedule. Here are the sections in each publication listing you should read:

*Publisher's statement.* In one paragraph, each publisher describes his magazine, its audience and editorial emphasis. Some will give you editorial content percentages. See if your choices feature new products, literature reviews, and application stories. This paragraph should give you enough of a summary so that you can view the details that follow in the listings with some understanding, even though you may never have seen the publication.

1. *Personnel* Look for the name of the editor, or editors, you want to reach.
2. *Representatives and branch offices* These are the locations of the space salespeople. Strictly speaking, their job is to sell advertising space, but most are willing to offer some suggestions to help you improve your chances of being picked.
13. *Special issues* In this section you will find whether the publication has regional or demographic issues, a buyer's guide, and other targeted issues.
16. *Issue and closing dates* Here you will find the publication dates and the latest dates on which advertising copy will be accepted. If you have timely news, the information in this section is important.
18. *Circulation* The information in this section will give you a picture of the mix of readers by territorial distribution as well as job function.

If you scan these headings, the job of evaluating the publications for your publicity list will be much easier.

In addition to trade magazines you will probably want to develop a list of local publications for your corporate publicity. Few industrial advertisers have enough customers close enough to the plant to warrant a strong product publicity effort in these publications. But there are other reasons for letting your neighbors know who you are, what you do, and how well you do it. Mainly, local publicity is a good way to build a steady flow of employment applications. Even though you may not be in need of people, you will get unsolicited résumés as your local public relations effort begins to pay off. Then, when you do need people, it's a lot easier to go to the résumé file than it is to advertise and be forced into filling a job on short notice.

If you have a direct mail program that includes addressing equipment, use the facilities to set up your publicity mailing list. Otherwise, simply set up the list on file cards so they can be typed quickly and easily when needed. And be sure to make changes in your list whenever necessary. Not unlike other business professionals, trade magazine editors move around quite a bit. Keep up with the editors to keep up your list. Some of the publications will send you notices of personnel changes, and others won't. To keep up with roving editors, have someone check the names on your list against the listings in SRDS every few months. It's a tedious job, but it's worth the effort. You don't like to receive a letter addressed to your predecessor do you? Editors feel the same way.

## HINTS TO HELP YOU GET PUBLISHED

No matter how well you write your release, and no matter how closely you follow the format preferred by industrial editors, the chances are that your copy will be edited. If nothing else, the material will be shortened to fit available space. It may be rewritten to conform to a publication's special style. And it could be changed to emphasize a pont the editor feels is more important to his or her readers than the point you decided to feature. But, for whatever reason, expect some editing.

When you anticipate editing, you can give your copy a better chance of survival if you make the editor's job easier. And the best way to do this is prepare your releases to conform to these guidelines.

1. Put your company name, address, and phone number at the top of the sheet. It's really best to have a sheet printed that not only identifies the company, but plainly states that this is a news release.

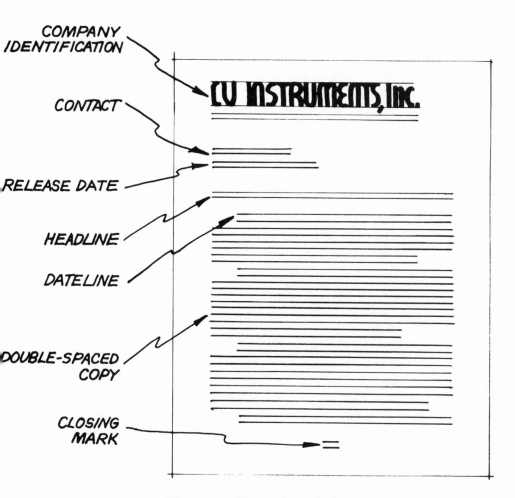

Figure 9-1   News release format

2. The name of the person at your firm for editorial contact should be included. You might want to provide more than one name here. The name of the person responsible for the preparation of the release should always be on the release, but you might also name the individual who has the technical responsibility. Quite often editors will call for additional information, and it can save time if the editor can go directly to the technical person. However, be sure to alert these people that they may receive calls and to be prepared for them. Also, you should have them tell you when they receive calls. It's a good idea to follow up with the editor who called, not only to make sure that he or she has everything that's needed, but to see if the interest is strong enough to make more out of the material than just a product release. Many a full-blown technical article has evolved in this manner.

3. The release date is next. This date tells the editor the date after which the release can be run. If it's important to you that the material appear in a specific issue, this is the place to make the point. However, most releases are sent out with this line: For Immediate Release. In effect, this tells the editor that he can use the material at any time. When the date states after such-and-such a date, the editor can assume that either the product is brand-new or is first appearing as exclusive feature material elsewhere.

4. Write a brief headline. Don't write an advertising headline, just straight exposition.

This will never do:

**Unique Pressure Regulator Outperforms Competitors and Features Twice the Corrosion Resistance**

This will do:

**Teflon-Lined Regulator Handles Sulphuric Acid and Delivers Flow Rates as Low as One Milliliter per Minute**

The first headline says nothing. What's unique? How does it outperform the competitive regulators and twice what corrosion resistance? The second headline is short, specific, and factual.

5. Begin your copy with a date line. This includes the place where the action took place plus the date on which the action occurred. You can skip the date for most product releases, but it should be included when you are sending out personnel and corporate news.

6. Double-space all the text. Never, never send single-spaced text to an editor. Not only is it more difficult to read than double-spaced text, it doesn't leave room for editing. Remember, your copy will be edited.

7. Write an opening paragraph that sums up the major points of the release. Try to tell who, what, when, where, why, and how in this paragraph. The text that follows will expand on the opening material.

8. Write the paragraphs that follow the opening in a descending order of importance. If the editor needs to shorten your text, he or she will probably just cut from the bottom, leaving the front matter intact.

9. If there is any literature describing the product, include it with the release and mention in the text that the literature is available.

10. Use a closing mark at the end of the release. Old-time telegraphers used the figure 30 to signal the end of a message, and this element is still acceptable. Some people also used "-end-" to tell the editor that there is no more. This may seem trivial, but if one page of a two-page release is lost, the editor may never get to some of the important points if he or she thinks the release is complete on a single sheet. If your text runs longer than one page, use the word "more," centered at the bottom of the page to indicate additional material follows.

11. Send a good quality 4 x 5 or 8 x 10 glossy, black and white photograph with your release. Stick to one size or

the other; publishers gang their halftone shots for economy. If they have to refocus for an odd-size picture, they are less likely to use it. Today, it appears that the 4 x 5 is the preferred size. They are less expensive for you to make in quantity, and the publisher can gang more of them on a sheet of film. Make sure the picture has good contrast. Most pictures are greatly reduced when they are printed, and a flat halftone will wash out in publication.

Identify each photograph with the name and model number of the product, the name and address of your company, and the name and phone number of the individual to contact within the firm. Don't write on the back of the photograph. The pressure from a pen or pencil will emboss to the surface and destroy the image. Type all the information on a label and attach it to the back of the print. See the chapter on photography for more information.

12. If you are sending releases to magazines that run some of their publicity in process color, be sure to include a transparency of the product. Most magazine production people prefer 4 x 5 material, but will consider a 2¼ x 2¼ inch transparency. Very few will touch a 35mm slide. If your original color picture was made with a 35mm camera, the image can be blown up by a commercial lab to 4 x 5 dimensions. It's worth it to get the color treatment that is usually in the front of the magazine.

13. If you happen to have color separations already made, consider offering them to an editor. Color separations are very expensive, and if you can save the magazine money, you will increase your chances of pickup. This material may have been made for your catalog, and can be adapted by the magazine for its pages.

14. When lawyers are asked to approve copy, they feel that they must give their clients their money's worth by insisting that all copyright and patent information be stressed. They're trained to protect, not to promote.

However, you can't expect editors to use patent and trademark registry information in the releases they publish for you. The owner of a trademark is expected to protect his or her property by the use of the mark, but it's unreasonable to expect others to be as zealous in its use.

15. If you are enclosing photographs with your release, include a piece of cardboard that is the same size as the inside of the envelope and place protective sheets of paper over the faces of the prints. It also helps to mark the word "photographs" on the front of the envelope.

Now let's see how to prepare each of the publicity pieces you are most likely to use.

## HOW TO PREPARE A NEW-PRODUCT RELEASE

Most people think of a product release only to introduce a totally new product. This is important, of course, but every change or modification of a product is news for the people who will buy it. However, don't try to wring more out of an editor than he or she is willing to give. Changing the knobs on your spectrophotometer from blue to red is hardly reason for an editor and your prospects to get excited. New options, accessories, and expanded specifications are newsworthy items.

Keep the text short. This doesn't mean that you have to leave out important information, only unimportant words. The unimportant words usually turn out to be adverbs and adjectives. They provide color in other writing, but their use in product publicity introduces vagueness. To say that a new linear amplifier has 1,000 watts peak envelope power says something. A new, high-power amplifier says nothing.

If you are going to overwrite, do it with the technical specifications. An editor can chop out that which is not too important to the readers.

If possible, include price information. When there is a basic unit that can be modified, or used with accessories, include the lowest price along with the prices of representative accessories.

# CU INSTRUMENTS, Inc.

223 Riverwood Road, Riverwood, NJ  07666      (201) 123-4567


CONTACT:  Robert J. Brown

FOR RELEASE:  After January 25, 1980


ROTATING SEAT ELIMINATES GALLING IN CORROSIVE SERVICE VALVE

Riverwood, NJ -- C.V. Instruments, Inc. has developed a valve with a rotating seat that eliminates damage caused by galling in conventional needle valves, regardless of the closing pressure applied to the handle.  The valve can be used with corrosive fluids such as sulphuric acid, and can be operated at pressures as high as 5000 psi.  It can be used with fluid temperatures as high as 450°F.

Called the CorroFlo, the valve requires less than ten foot pounds of torque to close at the maximum operating pressure. Once the rotating seat contacts the orifice in the valve body, it no longer turns as the handle is turned to complete the closure.

Available in sizes ranging from 1/4" to 3" NPT, the CorroFlo is made of 316 stainless steel and has a Teflon-lined cavity.

A product specification and application sheet is available.

-end-

Figure 9-2   News release copy


It's not always possible to include price, especially when the sale requires individual negotiation. But, whenever possible, prices are helpful for the editor as well as the prospects.

As I mentioned earlier, you should send your release to all publications you feel will be interested. However, the applications in different areas often require an explanation to the editor. Don't try to do this in the release. The release copy should stick to the product basics. The best way to handle the different markets is to include a supplementary sheet that describes where and how the product fits into the market served by the magazine. Don't go into great detail. Just stick to the facts. The editor won't publish the application information, but it will help him or her decide whether or not the product will be of interest.

## HOW TO PREPARE A NEWS RELEASE

There is usually very little space for general business news in trade magazines, so be sure that yours is important before you waste any time and money creating a release. However, it's often possible to get seemingly uninteresting news placed by phrasing the story from the readers' point of view.

For example, suppose you just doubled the size of your plant and want everyone to know about it. This, in itself, is ho-hum news for an editor dealing with fast-breaking technological developments. But, if you write your release around the benefits that will accrue to the readers of the magazine, your chances of publication will be much better. The building addition may allow you to double production of a product that is in short supply. From an editor's point of view, such information now is news. Look carefully behind all of your general news material for reader involvement, and avoid the horn-blowing aspects.

Corporate news usually has narrow appeal. That is, few people besides the editor of a foundryman's magazine, for example, will care that you have doubled your capacity to produce custom hollow cores. But the few editors who will be interested will probably be very interested. For this reason, you are usually better off tailoring your news stories to the specific needs of individual publications rather than broadcasting them to every magazine on your list. But, be prepared to answer a lot of questions if an editor shows interest. Product releases seldom require additional explanation, but business news often raises more questions than can be answered in a release. For this reason, you will probably be contacted by the editor or editors to whom you sent the release if they plan to run it.

Because of the nature of corporate news, you are better off contacting the editor by phone to discuss the story before you send out any material. If the editor is interested, he or she may want to cover the story rather than just use your release. When this happens, you will get much better coverage than you could hope for with just a pickup release. Many of the lead pieces in trade magazines start as editorial queries and blossom into feature material.

If you do your release for general distribution, follow the guidelines I outlined earlier, and write the piece to follow the style of a newspaper story. Start at the top with all the important information and amplify as you build the story. Writing news is like building a pyramid from the top down. Start with the important point and then build the supporting information. Watch out for superlatives and prune the sell. If you have any questions about style and don't want to take the time to read a book on journalism, read the material written by the editors of the top magazines. You can learn a lot just by seeing how they put together a story.

## HOW TO WRITE A FEATURE ARTICLE

Here's where editorial contact will be most important. It's not that your friendship with an editor will give you a special advantage; rather, it's only by working together that you can hope to be successful in placing feature articles. Simply mailing feature material to an editor is seldom successful. Editors prefer to have a hand in shaping the stories they publish.

Never write your article and then try to place it. There are just too many elements that must fall into place before feature material gets published. It's always best to start with an outline of the article and a one-paragraph summary. With this material, either phone or write the editor whose magazine you feel will be best for the story. This approach wastes the least amount of time for you and the editor, and will result in the best working conditions when the article is accepted.

Feature stories must fit in with the other stories that have been planned as well as with the editorial balance of the magazine. If you write your story in advance, and it doesn't fit exactly, the chances are that it will be rejected, rather than returned for revisions. However, if you contact the editor first with the idea, he or she may give you the go-ahead with specific suggestions for the development of the material. Or, the editor may assign a reporter to do the story.

If you get such an acceptance, be ready to offer whatever help the editor needs. Plant tours, demonstrations of the product in use, visits with satisfied users, and other such events are often requested when a feature story is being developed.

Unless the article is to be under the by-line of the editor, you should use the name of a person in the company who is most responsible for the material. Even though the engineer who developed the process you are publicizing can't put three words together to form a sentence, the story is his or hers. The public relations writer is best kept anonymous.

It's best not to take any pictures until the editor has worked on the story. Let him or her suggest what would be best for the piece. Your idea of what might be a good picture is probably too commercial for the editor, so ask for suggestions before you have any pictures taken.

The same is true of drawings. You may have the best draftsperson in the business, but some magazines routinely redraw every illustration to conform to their graphic standards. Before you have any drawings made, talk with the editor and determine just what is needed. Rough sketches may be just right, and the cost is small. You could waste time and money preparing finished artwork that will be redrawn.

It's not too difficult to decide which magazines will be appropriate for your new product releases, but it takes quite a bit of effort to get a match for feature material. You should be quite familiar with the type of material that has been published in the past, as well as the way in which it has been handled. The editorial content of some magazines, for example, is made up of a series of mini-stories and one feature article. Unless you've got the story of the year, your chances are probably better shooting for one of the mini-features.

Timing is critical. If you have a copy of the magazine's editorial calendar, as I suggested earlier in the chapter, you know when special issues will be coming up that will showcase your article. But be sure to contact the editor at least six months in advance with your article idea and outline.

You will reap considerable benefit from a published article. But don't let the benefit end with publication. Ask the editor for the right to reprint the story and send it along with product literature when you answer inquiries. Yes, even though you did the piece, the copyright belongs to the publisher, unless you arranged for it yourself and the publisher agreed. Usually it's just a matter of adding a line saying that the piece was reprinted by permission from the magazine, and then listing the date of the issue.

## HOW TO USE PUBLICITY TO OPEN NEW MARKETS

As I mentioned earlier, you should send your releases to every magazine that can conceivably reach a potential user of your product. And, if you send along the separate application information to the editor, you will increase your chances of publication. Magazine publishers are just as interested in seeing you develop a new market for your product as you are. If the market exists, and their publicity helped open it, you will probably use their magazine to expand the market with paid space.

Even when you send additional information to an editor, you may find it difficult to get your material published simply because there may be too much new in the field for products that are a direct fit. However, you can help yourself a lot by talking with the advertising space salesperson in your territory with a promise of advertising. Be honest and tell him or her that you want to see if there is a market for your product in the magazine. These requests seldom fall on deaf ears.

## WHO SHOULD CREATE YOUR PUBLICITY?

Creative writing this isn't. Yet, it requires good writing skills and journalistic discipline to translate technical data into readable English. There is a danger in using technically trained people who understand the product but can't write. And there are problems with the professional writer who doesn't understand technology.

You can find technical journalists in ad agencies, public relations shops, and working as free lancers. You may want to farm out the writing to an individual, but handle the placement yourself. Or, if the volume justifies it, hire a person to handle the work on a full-time basis. The largest single expense for a press release or feature story is the writing, unless the project involves extensive photography. However, if you can find a good individual or agency to handle your writing, it can take a lot of the load off your shoulders. Actually, the time spent in writing is usually less than that spent doing the research. Add it all up, and the time you or one of your employees spends away from other work may turn out to be an expensive trade-off. However, you can save quite a bit by handling all of the other details in-house.

Now do you see why I tried to intimidate you at the beginning of this chapter? A well-planned and implemented publicity program can do a lot for you. But you have to know what you are doing.

One final word of advice. Don't be afraid to edit your copy four, five, or a dozen times to get top material. The more experience a writer gets, the more he or she edits. It's only when you are a novice that you do little editing—not because your work is that good, but because you just don't recognize how terrible it is.

# Chapter 10

# Photography: How to Do It Yourself or Buy It for Less

Every part of an ad must pull its own weight. A good headline can be wasted in a poorly illustrated ad, and if the overall impression doesn't convey a selling idea quickly, you will have spent money for nothing. A lot of effort has gone into trying to determine whether people look at headlines or illustrations first, but little solid information is available on the subject. For your purposes, though, you should assume that neither is more important than the other, but if one is weak, your ad will be a loser.

The more interesting the illustration, the more effective the ad will be. Illustrations can be interesting from a subject matter point of view, or in terms of the illustration technique used. A well-conceived illustration does more than attract attention; it tells the reader something about the product, sets the tone for the copy, and sends the reader all sorts of unwritten messages. For example, illustrations can convey important selling points, such as ruggedness, adaptability, and quality. A picture of a jackhammer operator wearing an advertised watch tells the reader, without words, that the watch is rugged. The same watch worn by a model in a tuxedo says that the watch is the height of fashion.

## PHOTOGRAPHY OR ARTWORK?

Products can be illustrated in many ways—with photography or any number of different drawing techniques. The choice is governed by the impression you want to create and by the reproduction capability of the publication. For the advertiser of industrial products, however, photography is often the wisest choice. It's not that some products can't be rendered by an illustrator, or that there are no illustrators capable of doing justice to the product. It's just that a photograph portrays reality, and those who read ads in business, trade, and technical journals are reality-oriented people. You might commission the finest illustrator to render your pressure regulator, but some readers might think it doesn't exist because it wasn't photographed. This may seem like an oversimplification, but if you thumb through any trade magazine, you will find more photography in the ads than artwork. And you will probably find yourself more attracted to photographs of products, rather than drawings.

However, some of the most creative and successful ads I've seen have combined the reality of photography with imaginative layouts and supplementary artwork.

Good photographs have depth and tonal variations. And they can be reproduced by halftone engravings very well in most magazines. Wash drawings can also be reproduced well, but they lack the believability of a photograph. Photographs are especially important in ads that feature case histories or testimonials. They enhance the authenticity and believability of the copy. Photographs also create a feeling of immediacy. And, of course, people respond differently to various styles of illustrations. For example, I like pen and ink drawings, but am not especially fond of monochromatic wash renderings. However, good photographic style is appreciated by just about everyone. The art of the photographer doesn't get in the way of the message. The reader doesn't make artistic judgments, as might be done with a rendering. Rather, the message of the ad is perceived without perceptual noise in between. Remember that what I am saying applies mainly to industrial and trade advertising. High fashion depends heavily on artistic renderings, as well as photography.

The illustrator who works with a camera is as much of an artist as the person who creates a picture with brushes and paint. The truly creative photographer can use the camera to portray reality in novel and attention-getting ways. For example, the work done with super wide-angle lenses portrays the reality of the subject, but in creatively distorted ways that attract attention.

The reader of business and trade magazines is less interested in being entertained than in getting information, and the photograph is often more informative than artwork. Many industrial ads don't illustrate a product at all; they show the benefits of using the product.

## DO IT YOURSELF OR USE OUTSIDE PROFESSIONALS?

If you believe camera manufacturers' advertising, the photographer has little or nothing to do with the creation of a good photograph. Just point and shoot, they say. Don't you believe it. Excellent photographs can be made with an old Brownie in the hands of a person who knows how to take pictures. However, you can put the best Leica in the hands of a klutz and soon wish you had hired a professional for the job. But don't be discouraged. With some effort, you or someone in your organization can learn to take good photographs. The decision involves not only a cash commitment for equipment, but a personal commitment on the part of the person who will be taking the pictures.

If you start with an amateur shutterbug, make sure that the person realizes there is a big difference between winning camera club competitions and taking photographs that sell merchandise. Camera club competition success is only a bare beginning. If there are no formal classes in your area where commercial photography is taught, you, or your aspiring photographer, should read everything that has been written on the subject, subscribe to the professional magazines (not just those written for amateurs) and study ads created by the industrial giants to see how they handled their pictures. Looking at the work of others will show you what finished pictures should look like, but there's no way you can learn how to do it from this exercise. However, as you read the professional journals and books on the subject, the pieces will begin to fall into place. I can't give you the short course in a single chapter, but I can give you some help on how to select and use equipment. Let's start with the equipment that will be most useful.

## HOW TO CHOOSE THE BEST CAMERA FOR THE JOB

No one camera is the best for every job. The camera you buy should be selected because it will be most practical in most situations, or you should consider buying more than a single camera. Most people think first of a 35mm camera when they plan to do their own photography, but this may not be the best investment. The 35mm equipment is great if you must get lots of on-site shots of your products in action, or if you want to capture people for public relations purposes. But for most in-house product shots, other equipment is more practical. Let's look at the view camera first.

View cameras are big, bulky affairs, but when you master their use, there is little that can't be done with them, except chase visiting dignitaries around the plant for candid shots. Don't bother with 8 × 10 equipment, think about a 4 × 5 if you want the most flexibility for your product photography. These numbers refer to the dimensions in inches of the negative produced by the camera. The film is loaded in holders, one shot at a time, unlike 35mm and roll-film equipment, which can take many pictures with a single film-loading.

View cameras are used on tripods. The image you see on the ground glass on the back is inverted, and you must use a separate light meter to get the proper exposure. However, these tasks are relatively easy to learn if you have any interest in photography and want the best possible product shots. Perhaps the most important advantage of a view camera is its ability to correct for perspective problems. The lens board and the back of the camera, which is in the same plane as the film, can be tilted and swung independently to compensate for distortion factors, or to create them when you are aiming for a special effect. Most view-camera lenses can be stopped down to f64, which means that you will lose very little depth of field when you are shooting up close. This loss of sharpness in front of and behind the subject when the camera is up close is a serious problem with 35mm and some roll-film cameras.

Also, because of the large negative, your prints will be virtually grainless, even when very fast film is used. If you've ever looked at some prints that have been blown up from 35mm negatives, you have probably noticed that the image tends to get sandy or grainy. The image loses clarity under these conditions, but this is rarely a problem with the large negative of a view camera.

View cameras can be used with as many different types of lenses as can be used with a 35mm camera. But remember that lenses can only be used for the format for which they are designed. Because so many people buy and use 35mm equipment, most lenses for this format are relatively inexpensive, compared with the lenses that can be bought for view-camera equipment. You could pay more for a good wide-angle view camera lens than you might pay for a brand-new, top-of-the-line 35mm camera with a normal lens included.

Most professional photographers use view cameras extensively for their product shooting. And most pros have the darkrooms necessary to load the film sheets into the holders for use in the view camera. If you get a view camera, you will need a darkroom to load film into the slides. But, you will probably avoid using the darkroom for processing and printing.

Between the view camera and 35mm equipment, there are roll-film cameras that use 120-size film. The negative is either rendered in a square format of 6 × 6 centimeters (2¼ × 2¼ inches) or in a 6 × 9 centimeter format. This is smaller than the 4 × 5 inch negative you get from a view camera, but it still provides a large enough image so that all but the largest blow-ups will be sharp and not grainy.

Some 2¼ cameras have limited tilting capabilities to allow you to correct for perspective problems, but for the most part these cameras are limited to a single plane. The twin-lens reflex, as represented by the classic Rolleiflex, was a very popular camera a number of years ago. It's still a very good camera, but the twin-lens principle has given way to a single-lens body that allows you to view the subject through the same lens that will be used to take the picture. There are a number of advantages to this system; the most important for the in-house photographer is the elimination of the parallax problem inherent in the twin-lens system. Also, most of the newer single-lens reflex 2¼ cameras have much greater flexibility than their ancestors in many areas—faster shutter speed, electronic flash synchronization, and interchangeable lenses, to name just a few. The 2¼ format can be used to get good still-product shots, yet it is still usable as a candid camera. It's heavier and a little clumsier to use than a 35mm, but I think it represents the best investment if you are not going to get a view camera.

Incidentally, both the 4 × 5 view camera and some of the 2¼ equipment have adapter backs for Polaroid film. If you need pictures in a hurry, the combination of the sharp, fast lens on your studio equipment plus the instant picture capability make the purchase of the adapter a good investment. And you will find that the Polaroid adapter will help you make layout shots for your art director before the final pictures are made.

Some cameras are better than others, but the differences are often subtle, and the cost differentials great. Rather than settle on a brand of equipment because of its prestige value, I suggest that you select the camera that will give you the greatest flexibility. Choose a camera that has the most accessories that can be adapted to your needs, and that will be most practical for your own style of shooting. For example, some cameras mount their lenses to the body with threaded connections. This is time-consuming, and it's possible for the lens to unscrew and fall out. Others mount with a snap-on bayonet connection that is fast and safe. If you are concerned with safety and need to change lenses quickly, you might consider a camera with bayonet mounts. The point is that you should evaluate a number of cameras based on your needs and the features each offers.

## SELECTING LENSES

You can buy all manner of lenses for your camera, whether it's a 35mm, roll-film, or view camera. Which lenses will be most valuable? This can only be determined by your needs. However, to help you, here are some hints on the use of the three types of lenses.

### The Normal Lens

The normal lens is most often used because it gives coverage roughly equivalent to that of the unaided eye. Its focal length varies with the size of the film used. For example, in a 4 × 5 camera, the normal lens focal length is about 5¼ inches. The focal length of a normal lens used with a 35mm camera is about 50mm, or 2 inches, and it has a 45° angle of view.

The normal lens is most often used when you can get everything into the frame while standing in a convenient camera position. It's only for capturing subjects at greater distances, or when larger scenes are to be photographed from less than desirable positions, that other lenses become practical. There are other considerations, such as using longer or shorter focal lengths for special effects, but this use is beyond this book. However, be sure to read everything you can in both artistic and technical photography books about these lenses and their uses before you make any decisions.

### The Wide-Angle Lens

Wide-angle lenses give an image that is greater than that of a normal lens. Most common wide-angle lenses add about 30 degrees to the range of vision provided by normal lenses, and some special lenses can cover 160 degrees.

In general, wide-angle lenses give a greater depth of field than normal lenses at the same camera position. This can be important if you are shooting in close where the depth of field is short in a normal lens, and where you want everything in front of and behind the subject in sharp focus.

Wide-angle lenses can introduce distortion. For example, you've probably seen the photos of buildings that seem to come to a point, even though you know they are perfectly square. In some cases, this distortion is desirable, as when the art director wants to enhance size, or create a feeling or depth. However, if you want to render something as realistically as possible, the distortion common with wide-angle lenses can be a problem.

In some wide-angle lenses this problem has been corrected, but these are expensive. However, it's possible to correct for this distortion without special lenses when you use a view camera. The view camera, if you recall, is a large format affair in which the front lens board and the rear film back can be independently adjusted. These adjustments can be used to correct for distortion, or they can be used to create it.

## The Telephoto Lens

The telephoto lens magnifies the image much the same as a telescope would. There are many focal lengths of telephoto lenses for each format, and you may be confused when you first begin to look at the camera catalogs. For the 35mm camera, telephoto lenses begin at 85mm and range to over 1,000mm. The extreme lengths are of little value, unless you are interested in industrial espionage. Perhaps the most practical long or telephoto lenses are 85mm and 135mm. Both of these lenses will give quite a bit of flexibility, but I wouldn't buy both. My feeling is that the 85 is too close to a normal 50mm lens. The 135 is long enough to be very practical for getting shots of your products that may be mounted on some hard-to-get-at place.

Oddly enough, the optical characteristics of a mild telephoto lens, such as an 85mm, 105mm, or a 135mm lens for a

35mm camera, are perfect for portraiture. You can use a normal 50mm lens, but to get a decent-size image in the view finder, you have to work pretty close to your subject. Forget about using a wide-angle lens for head and shoulders portraits. Not only will you get some distortion, you will just about have to sit on your subject's lap to get the shot. However, with a mild telephoto lens, you can work at a distance that will be comfortable for you and your subject.

## LIGHTING EQUIPMENT

Lighting equipment will be necessary, whether you're going to shoot products in your in-house studio, or get grab shots of people for publicity purposes. However, the requirements of each are quite different.

You should consider good floodlighting equipment for your in-studio product shots. You will need several lights, as well as some reflectors. Most industrial products have many surfaces, angles, textures, and colors. Each of these requires special attention with lighting. If you used one light to illuminate something as simple as a box, for example, some of the sides would be well lighted and others would not be lighted at all. Considering that you have only a few stops lattitude with most film, you would find a perfect exposure on the lighted surfaces, but considerable underexposure on the unlighted surfaces. Depending on the visual complexity of the subject, you could use as many as four or five lights before each surface was properly illuminated. And you might need one or more lights just to kill the shadows thrown on the background by the illuminating lights.

Ordinary tungsten floodlights with good reflectors are perfectly adequate for most product photography. But, if you're going to use models, or do much portrait work, you will find the heat from these lamps too much to bear. Small high-intensity lamps can be used, but you might consider the use of electronic flash equipment. It's not enough just to buy a flash. This is like having a single tungsten floodlight. Light from a flash, even when its intensity is carefully controlled to give the proper exposure, is flat. That is, all surfaces exposed to the light are evenly lighted, and there is very little tonal gradation and modeling of the subject. And the surfaces not illuminated will be underexposed. You will need several slave flash units as well as some reflectors, such as the very practical bounce-light umbrella. If you buy electronic flash equipment, it's wise to get gear that includes modeling lights so that you can preview the lighting of the subject. And, it's necessary to get a light meter that responds to flash. This is a special unit, and a conventional light meter won't do.

## ADDITIONAL EQUIPMENT

Whether you buy a big view camera or a small 35mm, be sure that you get a good, sturdy tripod. It doesn't pay to scrimp here. A $1,000 camera on a $25 tripod is asking for an expensive accident.

You will need a cable release. This is a remote shutter-activating device that allows you to snap a picture at slow speeds on a tripod-mounted camera.

It's a good idea to get a UV (ultraviolet) filter for each lens and to keep them mounted all the time. This filter is just plain glass, optically ground, of course, but it will protect the surface of the lens under it. You can leave it in place whenever you are shooting black and white film, but you will have to remove it for color, or you will have color shifts on your prints or transparencies.

Many filters can be used with both black and white or color film. Their use is beyond the scope of this book, so I suggest that you read a good basic photo book for some ideas on how to use them creatively. See the Appendix for some books and courses that can be helpful. You can save yourself a bundle of money by buying some seamless background material. Get one roll each of black, white, and grey. Background material is especially important, unless you have an unlimited retouching budget. Most product shots are taken in the plant, and you know what a jumble that can be. If a retoucher has to sort your plant from your product with an airbrush and some careful hand painting, you might wish you had left the whole thing to an outside photographer.

## WHERE TO LOCATE YOUR PHOTO STUDIO

If you're serious about doing your own photography, you should dedicate one spot just for the purpose. It's really a big mistake to buy all the gear, and then use someone's office every time a shot has to be taken. For one thing, you'll spend more time cleaning up a place that is used for another purpose, and for another, you may find that there may be no space available just when a shot has to be made.

By having a studio, even if it's quite rudimentary, you will have everything in one place, ready to use when needed. Such a studio should be planned so that you can easily maneuver the product or people to be photographed, and you should be able to move the camera and the lights just as easily.

The studio should be big enough to work in comfortably. Floodlights get hot, wires can be tripped over, and cameras are easily overturned in cramped quarters. Do it right—give yourself plenty of working room.

Be sure that the room is clean, and that there is little likelihood of dust or oily vapors from the shop getting in. Grime is the enemy of photography equipment.

### What about a Darkroom?

Unless you're a giant corporation and plan to employ a number of people in your photography department, I advise that you use outside labs to do your processing. Just equipping a darkroom for color and for black and white can run into lots of money. Unless the lab is in daily use, the cost of chemicals that go bad just sitting still can be expensive. Think of a darkroom the same way you would think of buying a piece of production equipment. If it can't pay for itself, it doesn't belong in the building—even if you're an active amateur and looking for a write-off for your hobby.

## HINTS FOR TAKING GOOD INDUSTRIAL PHOTOGRAPHS

You'll never learn to take good pictures by reading this book—or any other book, for that matter. However, if you read several books on picture-taking and take a lot of pictures while you're reading, you should be able to take reasonably good pictures when you're finished. You might consider taking a course if one is available near you, or you might even enroll in one of the several excellent correspondence courses. But, remember, these courses are geared for the amateur who wants to make good snaps, or perhaps even try his or her hand at some creative art photography. The principles are the same. You will just have to adapt what you learn about shooting a vase of flowers to shooting a gate valve on a chemical reactor vessel. A good picture of the gate valve can be just as much a work of art as the shot of the flowers.

Once you have learned the principles of exposure and composition, you should concentrate on lighting. Lighting can make or break a picture. Good industrial photographs should have enough contrast to be interesting, and to reproduce well. Flat lighting is uninteresting, and usually reproduces as a washed-out grey picture.

If you have a big piece of equipment that can't be lighted with floods or with electronic equipment, you may have to resort to light painting. This is very tricky, but something you can learn if you take the time to work with it. To paint a subject with light, you first light as much of it as you can with conventional lighting. Meter the subject so you have a long exposure. Then, with the shutter open for a long timed exposure, you use a hand-held light to "paint" the areas that could not be reached with stationary lighting. On a very long exposure, you may even walk through the scene, and not be recorded. But, if you try this, move quickly, and don't stand still in one place.

## The Characteristics of a Good Photograph

A good photograph is uncluttered. Pick a view of the product that has little or nothing in the background that will detract from the image. Of course, if the background is important to the illustration, it should be included and shown as it relates to the product. Many industrial product shots end up silhouetted in advertisements. But even though some retouching is required for this, it's still best to shoot the picture against a neutral background, such as one of the seamless backgrounds I mentioned earlier.

A photograph should be sharp and distinct. Focusing is seldom a problem, but if you're shooting fairly close to the product, the range of sharpness in front of and behind the product may vanish quickly. This depth of field, as I mentioned earlier, can be controlled to some extent by shooting with the smallest aperture, f22 on most 35mm cameras, and f64 on some view camera lenses. Of course, if you're shooting beyond the focal distance of the lens, and it's focused on infinity, everything beyond the point will be in focus, and much of what is in the foreground will also be in focus if the lens is stopped down to a relatively small opening.

A picture of the product just sitting by itself is seldom very interesting. But a shot of the product in use, especially if there are some people in the picture, can usually be very arresting. You might also think of showing the product being made, or show part of the product in relation to the finished piece. A good photograph tells a story as much as the copy in the ad.

## USING PHOTOGRAPHY FOR MORE THAN ILLUSTRATING PRODUCTS

Local as well as national publications are often interested in the business activities of companies, and will use pictures of corporate executives when they run the stories. These corporate image pictures are best made with 35mm equipment, showing the individuals in settings that relate to the story.

You can also use your pictures, blown up, as backgrounds for your trade show exhibits, or as decorating themes for offices, conference rooms, and waiting rooms.

New products can be introduced by salespeople long before the product sheets or catalogs are available if they have just a typewritten sheet of the specifications plus a good glossy photograph to show to prospects.

You can also make use of your picture-taking capability to enhance an employee relations program. Use shots of individuals in your company newsletter, if you have one, or post their pictures and tell of their accomplishments on the bulletin board.

## STOCK PHOTOS

At times you may need or want more than just a picture of your product. You may need a shot of something special that relates to the product in some important way. For example, you may make tube fittings that are used on offshore drilling rigs, but your plant may be located thousands of miles from the nearest rig. You can get these pictures either from free lancers in the area who will take them for a fee, or you might be able to buy a stock photo of just what you need for less money.

Stock photos are pictures owned by individuals or companies that they will sell or rent to you. Renting a photo may seem odd, but this is really what the arrangement amounts to. For a fee, you are given the use of the picture for a specific use. You return the print and agree that it will not be used for anything other than the specified product.

Stock photos may cost as little as a few dollars or they can run into the hundreds, depending on the subject, its availability, and the intended use of the picture.

Most industrial advertisers who use stock pictures buy shots of specific backgrounds that are used to position their product in a specific setting. Those who sell stock photos will send you either a catalog of available pictures or a batch of actual prints for you to choose from. When prints are sent, you use the one you want and return it with the others, paying for the one-time use.

## Building Up Your Own Stock File

Most of you reading this book are probably involved with some type of industrial product or service. It's not easy to come up with good stock photos of cracking towers and analytical laboratories when you need them. Therefore, it's a very good idea to build your own file. You can do this easily if one of the cameras you bought is a compact 35mm. Pack it and take it with you on every business trip, or whenever you anticipate being in an area where background photos might be found. You must be careful, of course, of using pictures of subjects that belong to others if they would object to having their items used in your advertising. If you have such pictures, it's a simple matter to contact the firm owning the site to arrange for permission to use it. Not everyone responds favorably to such requests, but enough do so that it's usually worthwhile to carry your 35 whenever possible.

## MODEL RELEASES

Some people are very touchy about the use of their faces in advertising. Even though you may pay an employee's salary, you have no right to use his or her picture in your advertising without consent. To save yourself a lot of headaches, have every person in your photographs sign a model release *when the picture is taken*. It's better to do it at the time the picture is taken than later. You may never use the shot, but you will have the release on file to use whenever you see fit. Going back to a person later can often be a problem, especially if the person has left the company, and you desperately want to use the shot.

Here's the wording of a standard model release:

In consideration of $1.00 and other good and valuable consideration, receipt of which is hereby acknowledged as paid by _____, I state that I am over 21 years of age and I do hereby consent to the sale, publishing, reproducing, and/or use of my photograph for any purpose including advertising, displays, exhibitions, editorial illustration purposes, and trade, and I do hereby grant _____ permission to copyright said photograph, and all of the above-mentioned uses are granted without restrictions, reservations, or limitations whatsoever.

_____
Legal Signature

The subjects may not be willing to grant you everything that is stated in the release, and you can modify it to include only the use for which the picture is intended. However, most people who are not professional models are not likely to deny you the use of their picture by refusing to sign the release.

## KEEP UP TO DATE

Photography, even though you may be using it to portray an industrial product, is a creative activity, and unless you keep up with the trends your pictures may have the look of ten years ago. To prevent this, look at photographs in the ads prepared by the industrial giants. Analyze how the pictures were taken, and especially determine the idea of the picture. Ask yourself what message the picture is trying to convey. Envision how the techniques might be used to portray your products.

And be sure to read the popular as well as the professional photography magazines on a regular basis.

## HOW TO BUY PHOTOGRAPHY FOR LESS

If all of this discussion of focal lengths and f-stops makes you think you're better off leaving the picture-taking to someone else, there are a number of ways to insure that you will get good pictures—and good prices.

Before you engage a professional photographer to make pictures for you, insist on seeing his or her portfolio. If possible, try to see the pieces in which the photographs were used. Once you feel that you have a person with the technical and artistic skills to make good photographs, you should be sure that he or she understands your product and how it is used so it can be photographed intelligently. I suppose that there are some wedding photographers who understand mechanics and can portray a technical product intelligently, but I don't think there are very many of them.

A good industrial photographer should do more than simply take a picture of your product. He or she should be able to look at it and, after discussing it with you, decide how to portray it for selling purposes without having to be told. If, for example, your pH meter is the only instrument of its kind with a digital readout, the photographer who emphasizes the tip of the probe and not the readout doesn't understand your product. You will know this after a few minutes of conversation—I hope!

How much should a picture cost? I've used excellent photographers whose prices were quite low and I've met others who charge enormous fees for mediocre work. Don't be fooled by super salesmanship. Look at the pictures in the photographers' portfolios and ask for prices. After you have talked with several photographers, you should have an idea of the range of charges in your area. When you know the high and the low and can judge the great from the mediocre, you should be able to make an intelligent choice. But, when you decide on a photographer, don't haggle price with him or her. You are buying time and talent. If you think it's worth it, pay the bill. If not, choose another.

Photographers usually charge by the shot for studio work and by the hour, half-day, or day for location work. Some charge for time and materials separately, and others will give you an inclusive price. I think charging separately for time and materials is the better way. The photographer is not in the business of selling materials, he or she is selling the talent necessary to make good pictures.

Once you have found a photographer who does the kind of work you like and who understands your product and its application, let the photographer know that he or she will be doing all or most of your work. Most photographers will, under these circumstances, keep their charges down because they can anticipate a volume of work, and will have little or no selling cost built into the account. The photographer who charges on the basis of time will be charging less as he or she becomes more familiar with working with you and your products.

# Appendix

# Sources of Helpful Information

## ASSOCIATIONS

Advertising Research Foundation
    3 East 54th Street, New York, NY 10022
American Advertising Federation
    1225 Connecticut Avenue, N. W., Washington, DC 20036
American Association of Advertising Associations
    200 Park Avenue, New York, NY 10017. (This organization
    has published articles supporting independent agencies,
    and critical of house agencies. Anyone contemplating an
    in-house agency should read their material to get a clear
    view of both sides of the question.)
Association of National Advertisers
    155 East 44th Street, New York, NY 10017
Association of Publishers Representatives
    850 Third Avenue, New York, NY 10022
Business and Professional Advertising Association
    205 East 42nd Street, New York, NY 10017
Construction Equipment Advertisers
    111 East Wisconsin Avenue, Suite 1700, Milwaukee, WI
    53202
International Advertising Association
    475 Fifth Avenue, New York, NY 10017

Mail Advertising Service Association International
    7315 Wisconsin Avenue, Washington, DC 20014
Print Advertising Association
    10–64 Jackson Avenue, Long Island City, NY 11101
Promotion Marketing Association of America
    420 Lexington Avenue, New York, NY 10017

## BOOKS

Gardner, Herbert S.: *The Advertising Agency Business*, Crain Books, Chicago, 1976.
Holtje, Herbert F.: *Theory and Problems of Advertising*, McGraw-Hill, New York, 1978.
Lem, Dean Phillip: *Graphics Master 2*, Dean Lem Associates, Los Angeles, 1977.
Mandell, Maurice I.: *Advertising*, Prentice Hall, Englewood Cliffs, N.J., 1974.
Melcher, Daniel and Nancy Larrick: *Printing and Promotion Handbook*, McGraw-Hill, New York, 1966.
Messner, Frederick R.: *Industrial Advertising*, McGraw-Hill, New York, 1963.
Sawyer, Howard G.: *Business-to-Business Advertising, How to Complete for a $1-Trillion-Plus Market*, Crain Books, Chicago, 1978.
Wright, John S., et al.: *Advertising*, McGraw-Hill, New York, 1977.

## DIRECTORIES

*Advertising and Communications Yellow Pages*, New York Yellow Pages, Inc., 113 University Place, New York, NY 10003
*Bacon's Publicity Checker*, Bacon's Publishing Company, Inc., 14 East Jackson Boulevard, Chicago, IL 60604
*Business Press Cost Guide*, The Media Book, Inc., 75 East 55th Street, New York, NY 10022

*Canadian Advertising Rates and Data,* Maclean-Hunter, Ltd., 481 University Avenue, Toronto, M5W 1A7, Ontario, Canada

*Direct Mail List Bulletin,* Standard Rate and Data Services, 5201 Old Orchard Road, Skokie, IL 60076

*Graphic Arts Monthly Buyers Guide,* Technical Publishing Company, 666 Fifth Avenue, New York, NY 10019

*Leading Advertisers in Business Publications,* American Business Press, 205 East 42nd Street, New York, NY 10017

*Printing Trades Blue Book,* A. F. Lewis and Company, Inc., 853 Broadway, New York, NY 10003

*Standard Directory of Advertising Agencies,* Standard Rate and Data Service, 5201 Old Orchard Road, Skokie, IL 60076

*Standard Rate and Data Service,* 5201 Old Orchard Road, Skokie, IL 60077. (Separate editions are published for business publications, community publications, consumer and farm magazines, radio and TV stations, newspapers.)

## PERIODICALS

*Advertising Age,* Crain Communications, 740 Rush Street, Chicago, IL 60611

*Advertising & Publishing News,* Hagen Communications, 51 Upper Montclair Plaza, Upper Montclair, NJ 07043

*Adweek,* ASM Communications, 230 Park Avenue, New York, NY 10017. (Separate editions are published for the East, Midwest, West, and Southwest.)

*Agency Sales Magazine,* Manufacturers Agents National Association, P. O. Box 1687, Irvine, CA 92713

*Direct Marketing,* Hoke Communications, 224 Seventh Street, Garden City, NY 11530

*Industrial Marketing,* Crain Communications, 740 Rush Street, Chicago, IL 60611

*Marketing Communications,* United Business Publications, 475 Park Avenue South, New York, NY 10016

*Medical Marketing and Media,* Navillus Publishing Corporation, 1074 Hope Street, Box 4790, Stamford, CT 06907

*Potentials in Marketing,* Lakewood Publications, Inc., 731 Hennepin Avenue, Minneapolis, MN 55043
*Print Magazine,* R. C. Publications, Inc., 355 Lexington Avenue, New York, NY 10017
*Sales & Marketing Management,* Bill Communications, 633 Third Avenue, New York, NY 10017

## SEMINARS

The following organizations have offered seminars that are of interest to those planning and running house agencies. Contact them for specific topic titles and their schedules of presentation.

American Management Association, 135 West 50th Street, New York, NY 10020
Business & Professional Research Institute, 205 Nassau Street, Princeton, NJ 08540
Center for Direct Marketing, 3 Sylvan Road, Westport, CT 06880
Direct Mail/Marketing Association, Inc., 6 East 43rd Street, New York, NY 10017
Performance Seminars Group, 61 South Division Street, New Rochelle, NY 10801

## REPORTS, SERVICES, BIBLIOGRAPHIES

*Cahners Advertising Research Reports,* Cahners Publishing Company, 221 Columbus Avenue, Boston, MA 02116
*House Agency Check List: A Guide to Planning Your Own Advertising Agency,* James Peter Associates, Inc., Box 772 Tenafly, NJ 07670
*How to Make a Newsletter Work,* Tek-Mark, Inc., 223 Old Hook Road, Westwood, NJ 07675 (free)
*Laboratory of Advertising Performance,* McGraw-Hill Research, 1221 Avenue of the Americas, New York, NY 10020

*Marketing Reports,* Crain Communications, 740 Rush Street, Chicago, IL 60611

*Media Data Forms,* Media Comparability Council, 1800 Pickwick Avenue, Glenview, IL 60025

*Media Planning and Management Kit: Strategy, Forms and Procedures for Business-to-Business Advertisers,* James Peter Associates, Inc., Box 772 Tenafly, NJ 07670

*100 Books on Advertising,* University of Missouri School of Journalism, 108 Journalism Building, Columbia, MO 65201

*Product Publicity Checklist: How to Tell Your Story and Get It Published,* James Peter Associates, Inc., Box 772, Tenafly, NJ 07670

# Index

ABC statement, 133-136
Addressing systems, 154
Advertising:
  competitors, 138
  definition, 165
  frequency, 126
  institutional, 148
  major goals, 124
  readership, 128
  repeated, 140
  responses, 140
*Advertising Age*, 103
Advertising agency, economics of
  running, 3-6
Advertising Directions, 9, 23
Agricultural Publishers
  Association, 25
*Advertising and Publishing
  News*, 3
American Association of
  Advertising Agencies, 15, 22,
  28
American Business Press, 25
American Management
  Association, 23
American Newspaper Publishers
  Association, 22, 25
Art:
  how to buy from professionals,
    121-122
  prices, 121-122

Audit Bureau of Circulations,
  132, 133, 134

*Bacon's Publicity Checker*, 169,
  171
Badger Company, 11, 18, 25
Binding, 56
Bleed advertisement, 130
Blue M Manufacturing Company,
  11, 23
BPA statement, 135, 136
Braithwaite, Rich, 12-15, 57
*Business Press Cost Guide*, 132
Business and Professional
  Advertising Association, 103,
  133

Cahners Publishing Company, 2
Cameras, how to select, 190-193
Christian, Richard, 28
Circulation:
  controlled, 126, 135
  how to evaluate, 132-136
Classified advertising, 130-131
Closing dates, magazines, 131
Coleman, Ron, 3
Collateral services, 27-29
Commissions, 1-2, 13, 19-22,
  26-27, 129
Compensation, agency, 3-4
Consent Decrees, 22, 25

Copy:
  audience for, 81-82
  benefits, 83
  central selling idea, 75
  cost, 102
  features, 83
  how to focus attention, 78-80,
    96
  how to write, 91-95
  length, 92
  objectives, 81
  product characteristics, 82-83
  seven key questions, 76-78
  style, 84
  ten step plan, 80-84, 96-97
  theme, 84
Copyfitting, 119
Copy regulations, magazine, 131
Copywriters:
  characteristics of, 100-102
  free-lance, 99-102
  sources of, 102-104
Cost-per-inquiry, 126, 128
Cost-per-thousand, 126

Die cutting, 34-35, 38
Direct mail:
  booklets, 160
  brochures, 160
  catalogs, 159-160
  copy length, 157
  equipment, 161
  folders, 159
  format, 157-161
  gimmicks, 160-161
  goals, 144-148
  judging, 148-149
  letter, 158
  newsletters, 160
  postal class, 162
  postal services, 156-157
  successful techniques, 162-164

*Direct Marketing,* 104
Direct response cards, 141
Discount, cash, 129-130
Dixey, George, 11, 23

Editorial relations, 167-171
Editorial statement, 136

Feature article, 182-184
Fees, 5, 13
Financial strategy, 7
Flat-bed cylinder letterpress,
  35-36
Flexography, 46
Fractional space, 3
Full service agency, 15

General Electric, 6, 8
Goals, 7, 9
Good client, how to be, 29-30
*Graphic Arts Green Book,* 69
Gravure, 43-44

Halftones, 46-48, 120
Headlines:
  attention-getting, 84-85
  benefits, 86
  command, 89-90
  how-to, 87-88
  length, 87
  news, 88
  picture integrating, 88-89
  prediction, 89
  problem, 85
  seven types, 87
  short story, 90
  testimonial, 90
  understandable, 86
House organs, 160

Independent agency, advantages
  of, 6, 14-16

*Industrial Marketing,* 6, 18, 103
Information gathering, 147
In-house agency:
    advantages, 6, 14, 15-16
    affiliate company, 23, 25
    growth, of, 13-14
    history, 18-20
    how to form, 22-25
    legality of, 17-18
    success characteristics of,
        10-12
Insertion order, 139-140
Inserts, 130
Issue dates, magazine, 131

Layout:
    balance, 111-114
    color, 118
    comprehensive, 110-111
    consistency, 116
    emphasis, 118
    finished, 109-110
    how used, 118-120
    motion, 115-116
    preparation, 106-111
    principles, 111-118
    rough, 108
    thumbnail, 107
    white space, 117-118
Lenses:
    normal, 193
    telephoto, 194-195
    wide angle, 193-194
Letterbooks, 146
Letterpress printing, 33-39
Lever Brothers, 19
Lewis Company, A. F., 69
Lewis, Gary, 20
Liability, 26-27
Lighting equipment, 195-196
List purge mailing, 155
Lithography, 39-43

Magazines:
    special issues, 140
    special services, 131
Mailing list:
    broker, 150-151
    brokerage commission, 152
    rental, 150-152
    selection, 152-153
    selectivity, 151
    updating, 153-155
Markets, new, 184
Mark-up, 5
Marsteller, Inc., 28
Mechanical requirements,
    magazine, 131
Mechanicals, offset, 41
Media:
    evaluation, 126-127, 129-132
    planning psychology, 127-129
    program management, 138-140
    recognition, 25-26
    strategy, 124-125
Media Comparability Council,
    133
*The Media Book,* 132
Monsarrat, John, 15
Moonlighters, 121

Negatives, mailing, 120
New product release, writing,
    179-181
News, corporate, 181
News release:
    copy, 180
    format, 175
    headline, 176-177
    how to prepare, 181-182

Offset:
    characteristics of, 41-43
    copy preparation, 41
    proofs, 48-49

Offset (continued):
  sheet fed, 40-41
  web, 41
Overhead, 7

Paper:
  folding, 56-58, 64-65
  glossy, 64
  grain, 65
  how to select, 53-55
  job lots, 65
  sizes, 54, 64
  trimming, 56
  types, 53-54
People, creative, 8-10
Periodical Publishers
  Association, 25
Per-job services, 28
Photographs, how they are
  printed, 46-48
Photography:
  accessory equipment, 196-197
  characteristics of good, 199
  choosing, 188-189
  darkroom, 197-198
  do-it-yourself, 189-190
  how to buy, 202-204
  how to take, 198
  model release, 201-202
  professional, 189-190
  stock, 200-201
  studio location, 197
  use of, 199-200
Plate, letterpress, 33
Plate, lithographic, 39
Platen press, 34-35
Primary audience, 127
Printer, how to select, 66-69
Printing:
  alterations, 61
  claims for defects, 62
  climate control, 66-67

color, 48
  conditions of copy, 60
  costs, 70-71
  delivery conditions, 61-62
  experimental work, 60
  fourteen ways to save money
    on, 62-66
  how to negotiate a fair price,
    69-71
  in-house, 71-73
  invoices, 62
  lowest bidder, 69
  order cancellation, 61
  overruns, 61
  ownership of proprietary
    materials, 60
  proofs, 60-61
  processes, 32-33
  protection of customers'
    material, 61
  quotations, 59
  split fountain, 65
  trade customs, 60-61
  underruns, 61
*Printing Trade Bluebook*, 69
Products:
  selling by mail, 146-147
  seven key questions, 95-96
Profit and loss responsibility, 7
Prospects, locating, 144-146
Publicity:
  costs, 166
  definition, 165
  editing, 185
  getting published, 174-179
  lists, 171-174
  who should create, 185
Pulver, Robert, 6, 8, 17, 24

Rates, space, 130
Reach, media, 126

Readership, how to evaluate, 136-138
Records, media, 140
Responsibilities, job, 9
Rotary letterpress, 36-38

Sales call, how to enhance, 146
Sample, mailing, 145
Santa Fe Industries, 9, 23
Screen Printing, 45
Special issues, 131
Special position, 130
Split run, 131
Standard Industrial Classification, 151
*Standard Rate and Data Service,* 120, 125, 128, 129, 136, 152, 169, 171
Steelcase, Inc., 20
Success, criteria for, 12-14
Suppliers, favored, 4-5

Tektronix Information Display Division, 12

Thermography, 46
Tipple, Fred, 23, 24
Trade show registrants, 150
Type:
    classifications, 49-50
    designing with, 51-53
    leading, 119
    selection, 119
Typography, 48-53

Velox prints, 41, 120
Verified Audit Circulation Corporation, 132-133, 135

Warner Lambert, 19
Woodburn, W. D., 9

Young, R., 11, 18, 25

Ziegenhagen, M., 10
ZIP Codes, 151

## About the Author

Bert Holtje has been president of Tek-Mark, Inc., an industrial advertising agency for more than 20 years. He is the author of 23 books including: *Theory and Problems of Advertising, Theory and Problems of Marketing, The National Directory of Manufacturers Representatives,* and *The Photographer's Business Handbook.* He has worked as a copywriter and an advertising director, is a member of the American Psychological Association, and holds a master's degree in psychology.